VILFREDO PARETO

WITHDRAWN

Masters of Social Theory
Volume 5

MASTERS OF SOCIAL THEORY

Series Editor:

Jonathan H. Turner, *University of California, Riverside*

This new series of short volumes presents prominent social theorists of the nineteenth and twentieth centuries. Current theory in sociology involves analysis of these early thinkers' work, which attests to their enduring significance. However, secondary analysis of their work is often hurried in larger undergraduate texts or presented in long scholarly portraits.

Our attempt is to provide scholarly analysis and also to summarize the basic, core idea of the individual master. Our goal is to offer both a short scholarly reference work and individual texts for undergraduate and graduate students.

In this series:

HERBERT SPENCER by Jonathan H. Turner, *University of California, Riverside*

EMILE DURKHEIM by Robert Alun Jones, *University of Illinois, Urbana-Champaign*

MAX WEBER by Randall Collins, *University of California, Riverside*

ALEXIS DE TOCQUEVILLE by Whitney Pope, *Indiana University, Bloomington*

VILFREDO PARETO by Charles H. Powers, *Santa Clara University*

Forthcoming volumes and their authors include the following:

GEORGE HERBERT MEAD by John D. Baldwin, *University of California, Santa Barbara*

KARL MARX by Richard P. Appelbaum, *University of California, Santa Barbara*

VILFREDO PARETO

Charles H. Powers

Masters of Social Theory
Volume 5

Cover Photo Courtesy of The Pareto Fund

SAGE PUBLICATIONS
The Publishers of Professional Social Science
Newbury Park   Beverly Hills   London   New Delhi

To my wife Joan,
with all my love

For information address:

SAGE Publications, Inc.
2111 West Hillcrest Drive
Newbury Park, California 91320

SAGE Publications Inc.
275 South Beverly Drive
Beverly Hills
California 90212

SAGE Publications Ltd.
28 Banner Street
London EC1Y 8QE
England

SAGE PUBLICATIONS India Pvt. Ltd.
M-32 Market
Greater Kailash I
New Delhi 110 048 India

Printed in the United States of America

Library of Congress Cataloging-in-Publication Data

Main entry under title:

Powers, Charles H.
  Vilfredo Pareto.

  (Masters of social theory ; v. 5)
  Includes index.
  1. Pareto, Vilfredo, 1848-1923.   2. Sociology—Italy.
I. Title. II. Series.
HM22.I56P356 1986   301'.0945   85-30456
ISBN 0-8039-2284-1
ISBN 0-8039-2285-X (pbk.)

FIRST PRINTING

Contents

Series Editor's Introduction

The work of Vilfredo Pareto remains an enigma to most contemporary sociologists, even social theorists. This book should, I feel, familiarize sociologists with the power of Pareto's approach and, as a result, give Pareto his proper due as one of the great masters of sociological theory. It is true, of course, that Talcott Parsons and even his nemesis, George Homans, both claimed to have derived inspiration from Pareto's work, but by their selective use of Pareto, they often obscured rather than clarified his contribution. Thus, Pareto's ideas need a proper airing, for more than any of his contemporaries at the turn of the last century, Pareto had a vision of sociology as a natural science, and he developed some of its basic laws. Yet, his important contribution to the cumulation of knowledge remains only vaguely appreciated.

Part of the reason for this situation is that Pareto's conceptual vocabulary was very awkward. Terms like *derivations, residues, sentiments, lions,* and *foxes* are, to say the least, rather odd for a natural science of society. Another reason for our failure to appreciate Pareto stems from the title used in the original English translation of his general sociological treatise, *The Mind and Society.* Such a title is hardly inspiring and rather absurd when one recognizes that Pareto's social theory is primarily macro in focus. Still another reason for the misinterpretation of Pareto is that some of his most important theoretical statements have only recently been translated. Thus, I do not feel that Pareto has been given a fair hearing by present day sociologists. And so, I am delighted that this volume of the Sage Masters of Social Theory series provides us with by far the best summary, interpretation, and analysis of Pareto's theories to date.

As with other authors in this series, Charles Powers sees the personal biography of a scholar as critical. Pareto came to sociology rather late in his life, after making significant contributions to the development of mathematical economics. In fact, many of his ideas, such as "Pareto Curves," are still an important part of modern economic analysis. The reasons that he left economics and gravitated to sociology are still relevant: Economic processes do not operate in a vacuum; they are impeded within a social, cultural, and political environment. Economics has, unfortunately, not heeded Pareto's advice, but contemporary sociologists who are now venturing into formal economic analysis can profit greatly from the lessons in Pareto's abandonment of economics for sociology. Pareto brought from economics important analytical tools, such as equilibria and cycles, as well as a faith that a formal science of sociology could be developed through the development of abstract models and principles on the interrelated dynamics of economic, political, and cultural processes.

All of the basic elements of Pareto's approach are presented and illustrated in the chapters to follow. Much of the seemingly vague terminology of Pareto's sociology is clarified; and even the more popular portions of his work, such as the "circulation of elites," are placed within a broader view of human social organization. Powers has thus provided us with much needed and timely reappraisal of Vilfredo Pareto. And I hope that this short book will rekindle interest in Pareto's approach to sociological theorizing.

Laguna Beach, California   —*Jonathan H. Turner*

Acknowledgments

Over the years, many people have encouraged and supported my work on Pareto. First among these is Jonathan Turner, who in the fall of 1977 urged me to read carefully *Treatise on General Sociology*. Five years earlier, Norbert Wiley imparted a healthy curiosity about Pareto (stimulated at the time by my reading of Joseph Lopreato's *Vilfredo Pareto: Selections from His Treatise with an Introductory Essay*), and it was under Professor Turner's direction that I pursued this interest. Jon gave me his most precious gift, the gift of time. We spent many long hours discussing Pareto's work, with Jon serving as a sounding board as I clarified my own thinking and developed my own interpretation of Pareto's theories.

In the same spirit of close, sustained, fruitful collegial association, I must also mention Renata Girola. Our collaborative effort to produce an English edition of *The Transformation of Democracy* provided a special opportunity for me to refine my grasp of the socioeconomic and political implications of Pareto's theoretical scheme.

There are a number of people I have interacted with less regularly but who have nonetheless contributed in important ways to this book. These are people who have provided critical feedback at important times, as well as encouragement to continue with my analysis of Pareto's ideas. They include Randall Collins, Juergen Backhaus, Reza Maghroori, David Heise, William Corsaro, Robert Robinson, Jerald Hage, Maurice Garnier, Martin Weinberg, Larry Cohen, John Stanley, and Susan Bechtel Allen.

Many people either helped in the actual preparation of the manuscript or strove to provide me with a conducive environment in which to work. In this regard, my special thanks goes to William Fellows Hunter, Timothy Saul, Al Goodyear, Mitch Allen, Eric Wright, John Davey, Wayne McGlothlin, Festus Crum, F.W. Andrews, and David Strange.

9

Final thanks go to Transaction Books for permission to quote from *The Transformation of Democracy* (Charles Powers, ed.) and to the Pareto fund for permission to quote from Pareto's *Treatise on General Sociology*.

Introduction

Frank Westie is fond of pointing out that most scholars hope for a kind of immortality. They want to be known in their lifetimes, and remembered thereafter, as people who have made appreciable contributions to cultural enrichment, the advancement of science, or the relief of human suffering. But few of us attain these lofty ends. Most people are known by only a few even in their own lifetimes, and most of us are completely forgotten by all but family members within a short time after our passing.

There is something tragic and lamentable in all this. It is nevertheless the fate most people must be prepared to accept. And yet, on rare occasions, a creative thinker makes such a profound impact that he or she cannot be ignored, even by subsequent generations. Vilfredo Pareto was one such person (as were the other sociological theorists assessed in this Sage monograph series). Pareto pioneered whole new methodologies for social scientific investigation, including the use of mathematical equations to model social dynamics and the use of social indicators to measure variables that are not directly observable. He also provided us with one of the most widely used and thought-provoking heuristic devices of the social sciences: the concept of "social system." And Pareto's works spawned entire bodies of research literature on the distribution of income, social welfare policy, social change, and political leadership.

By any objective reckoning, Pareto was an important figure in the early development of sociology, economics, and political science. This is, in itself, sufficient justification for a book of this nature. However, the contemporary relevance of Pareto's theories should not be overlooked. More than six decades after his death, scholars continue to read his work because it reveals important lessons about the social structural dynamics that have operated throughout human history. This quality makes Pareto's work timeless. In particular, Pareto has a great deal to say about the conditions that promote the economic growth and the sociocultural vitality of a nation.

This book presents a studied interpretation of Pareto's theory. The topics Pareto investigated and the examples he used are extensively employed, as are some quite similar but more contemporary examples, in order to give readers the flavor of Pareto's works in their original form. But this book also moves beyond Pareto. Insights and theoretical principles that are only suggested or hinted at in Pareto's original work are here made explicit and exact. Pareto fell short of his expressed goal of articulating a formal theory of society. Yet, a formal theory of society does suggest itself to me and is the core of the chapters to follow. Hence, this monograph is an attempt both to summarize and complete Pareto's work. Every effort is made to realize two objectives simultaneously: (a) to relate accurately the content and flavor of Pareto's work, and also (b) to isolate the social scientific principles that Pareto sought to discover but was never able to clearly arrive at on his own. This formal theory of social systems is, I believe, the fulfillment of Pareto's mission.

1

Vilfredo Pareto
A Personal Profile

Every great thinker stresses certain central ideas. These recurrent themes are like the woof and warp in a tapestry. They constitute the basic fabric of a theorist's argument. Focusing on them helps us to understand the analytical framework being advanced and the worldview being presented.

The worldview of every theorist is affected by personal biography. Each person's thoughts and concerns are shaped by family and historical background factors, the general qualities of the environment one is raised in, life traumas, and personal experiences. So beginning with a historical profile should aid us in identifying the important themes that recur in Pareto's work.

However, great caution is to be exercised. The unique experiences, idiosyncratic moods, trepidations, needs, and peculiarities of great thinkers are of little scientific interest in themselves. Their study merely serves as a starting point by setting the stage for our initial investigation. This first chapter, containing a treatment of background factors, will therefore be succinct. It begins with a brief biographical sketch and then moves forward to outline some of the philosophical presuppositions that Pareto seems to have retained as intellectual cargo.[1]

BIOGRAPHICAL SKETCH

There are at least three important factors to consider in a biographical sketch. These are family background, life experiences, and
psychological profile. Each is briefly examined in the passages that
follow. We will then go on to consider the conceptual themes and
theoretical issues that emerged from this blend of biographical factors.

General Family Background

Vilfredo Frederico Damaso Pareto's ancestors came from the vicinity
of Genoa, Italy. Genoa was founded in the eighth century B.C. and is the
site of a good natural harbor. The town was a commercial center by the
fifth century B.C., trading with the Greeks, Phoenicians, and Etruscans.
From the third century B.C., it was an important outpost in the Roman
imperial system. Consequential enough to be saved when barbarians
overran the rest of Italy, Genoa was successfully defended by Byzantine
General Belisarius and remained a mercantile outpost of the Eastern
Roman Empire until the middle of the sixth century A.D., when
Byzantium entered a period of geopolitical contraction.

The fortunes of Genoa declined after its defeat by the Lombards, and
the city's power receded until the tenth century when it was repeatedly
plundered by Saracens. But in the years that followed, Genoa regained
strength and the Genoese began their own materially profitable raids on
Muslim centers in the Mediterranean. Genoa became a hub of
commerce, ship building, banking, and cartography, and profited
heartily by playing a major transportation and communications role in
the Crusades. The city spawned colonies and trade stations as far away
as India and the Black Sea and was constantly battling against one
commercial rival or another.

Genoa was eclipsed by Venice in the fourteenth century and
dominated by France and Milan after 1398. During the sixteenth
century, Genoa became the banking center of Catholic Europe, thanks
to an alliance with Spain. (Columbus, it might be noted, was Genoese.)
Run as a quasi-republic governed by the equivalent of a chamber of
commerce, the major families thrived and exercised guiding hands over
social, economic, and political policy. But the independence of Genoa
was in perpetual danger. The city was bombarded by the French in 1684
and invaded by the Austrians in 1746. It lost its last colony (Corsica) to
the French in 1768, and it was occupied by Napoleon in 1796, blockaded

by the Austrians in 1800, and ceded as a war prize to Piedmont in 1815.

Pareto's ancestors were prominent merchants throughout this period and seem to have had a decided bent toward political activism. Involving themselves in the issues of their times, they wielded considerable authority. Giovanni Lorenzo Bartolomeo Pareto, Vilfredo's great-great-great-grandfather, was ennobled as a Marquis in 1729. A Marquis ranks just below a Duke in the aristocratic hierarchy of Europe. This is a title that Pareto was to inherit, and it is a vivid indication of the social standing and prestige members of the Pareto family enjoyed in Genoa. This, it should be noted, was a republican Genoa, operating within the French sphere of cultural influence, struggling to maintain its independence from all, and above all, fiercely antagonistic toward Austria.

As avid participants in the political arena, members of the Pareto family were intimately involved in the heated debates of their times. Pareto's grandfather and grand uncles were ardent republicans, and they were placed in important administrative positions during the Napoleonic period. Their fortunes may have suffered somewhat after the fall of Napoleon, but their republican sentiment apparently did not wane, even after the Republic of Genoa was ceded as a war prize to the House of Savoy.

Republicanism reached a fever pitch in the following generation. In Genoa, during the 1830s, Giuseppe Mazzini mobilized resistance against rule by Piedmont's royal House of Savoy. A republican activist, Vilfredo's future father (Vilfredo was not yet born), the Marquis Raffaele Pareto, was forced to flee from Italy for exile in France.[2] It was here that Raffaele Pareto married a French Calvinist named Marie Mattenier. They had two daughters and one son. Vilfredo Pareto was born on July 15, 1848, rue Guy, La Brosse, Number 10, Paris.

Life Experiences

The Marquis Raffaele Pareto was an exile without financial resources and had to be self-supporting. He was a successful hydrological engineer. In point of fact, Raffaele was regarded by his contemporaries as quite remarkable, and he published a number of important articles on hydraulics. Never rich, Raffaele Pareto nevertheless afforded his children the advantages of a reasonably affluent middle-class upbringing. Vilfredo received a quality education, and his parents seemingly imparted the values of hard work and moderate living to their children.

Raffaele Pareto, a conservative man by inclination despite his youthful republican activism, was eventually able to return to Italy where he settled in Turin. This may have been in 1854, although the exact date is in dispute. His wife and children followed sometime prior to 1859. Vilfredo continued his education, completing a degree in engineering at the Polytechnic Institute of Turin in 1869. Pareto finished first in his graduating class, just ahead of his friend Galileo Ferraris, who went on to make important scientific discoveries in his research on electricity.

Raffaele Pareto, by this time a civil engineer employed in the Piedmont bureaucracy, was transferred to Rome immediately following national unification in 1871. Vilfredo Pareto accompanied his parents and procured a job (like his father) as a civil engineer with the government-owned railway department.

Other engineering positions followed. Vilfredo Pareto was transferred to Florence in 1872. In 1874, he accepted a position as superintendent of Societá Ferriere Italiana where he remained for several years. This industrial concern operated a number of ventures including mining and ironworks in the Valley of the Arno. While with this firm, Pareto had a number of occasions to travel to England and Scotland on business, where he was enthralled by laissez-faire economic doctrine and the apparent success of British government policies promoting free-market operations.

This was an especially rewarding time in Pareto's life. He made influential friends and was admitted to the circles of the highly respected intelligentsia of Florence. Among other things, he turned his attention to the classics. Learning Greek, Pareto enriched himself by cultivating a knowledge of literature and history. He was also an active member in the Adam Smith Society and contributed commentary to the newsletter of that society and to the bulletin of the Academy of Geography in Florence. Pareto also dabbled in politics for a period. But he became more retiring after losing a bid for a seat in parliament in 1881 and after his father died in 1882. He continued to work in an engineering and managerial capacity, and occasionally contributed political commentary for various journals.

Pareto married a Russian woman, Dina Bakunin, in 1889.[3] They were able to retire to Villa Rosa in Frisole and live a marginally comfortable existence on consulting fees.[4] Madame Bakunin apparently enjoyed the life of a socialite. This was not altogether in Pareto's character but he indulged her as much as he could. He also began publishing commentaries and reviews at an amazing rate. Pareto's political commentaries attracted a considerable amount of attention, which was not entirely positive. Some of his public speaking engagements are said to have been shut down by Italian police, and he was harassed by thugs believed to be on a government payroll.

Most of Pareto's work at this time was polemic.[5] He argued in favor of free trade and open competition and assailed government interventionism. He maintained that protective tariffs, support subsidies, and government-granted monopolies hurt poor people by fostering inefficiency and encouraging the production of inferior products at high prices. It was Pareto's contention that government inhibition of free-market operations saps national strength by allowing uncompetitive firms to flourish and dominate the economy.

But Pareto was more than a polemicist. He was an engineer and a mathematician by training. It was only natural that Pareto's approach to the study of political economy should be flavored by his mathematical predilections and by his instincts as an engineer. In 1891, he began to publish papers translating economic theories into succinctly stated verbal propositions and mathematical formulas. This was a turning point. European economists (especially Maffeo Pantaleoni, who was later to become one of Pareto's most trusted friends) took immediate note, and this led to Pareto's appointment as Professor of Political Economy at the University of Lausanne in 1893.

Pareto distinguished himself in his early years at Lausanne and came to be known as "the father of mathematical economics" in recognition of the breakthroughs he made during that period. When Pareto was just breaking into his stride as an academic economist, he happened to inherit a great deal of money. This was in 1898 when an uncle died, making Vilfredo a major beneficiary. The financial independence provided by this inheritance was just what Pareto had always longed for. He purchased a quiet country villa in Céligny, Canton de Genève, where he could work in peace. It was, interestingly enough, after that point that he began making his most important contributions. Almost everything that we remember Pareto for was written at Céligny, including his masterpiece in economics *Manual of Political Economy* (first edition 1906, significantly revised second edition 1909). But it was also a period of some personal distress. After being abandoned by his wife in 1901, Pareto was joined by Jane Régis (born 1877) who became a lifetime companion, true love, and eventual wife.

By this time, Pareto was an accomplished and highly acclaimed economist. But he was deeply troubled by the narrow path being followed by his contemporaries in economics. He boldly argued that economic events can only be understood in terms of the broad sociopolitical contexts in which they occur. Rebuffed for these views, Pareto charted an independent course and began writing articles on sociology, a science he believed would incorporate into a single framework the previously separate studies of economics, politics, and public values, sentiments, and culture.

Notwithstanding Pareto's sincerity and hard work, he was sometimes ridiculed as an eccentric. Undaunted, he began writing sociological essays. Upon retirement, he devoted full energy to writing the massive sociological tome for which he is best remembered by sociologists and political scientists. Most of this work (largely completed by 1914) was written during a period of self-imposed isolation. Removing himself from free and open commerce in ideas, Pareto remained at his country villa, seldom venturing into urban centers and entertaining visits from only a few close friends. This is the theorist we remember as "the lone thinker of Céligny." The final years of his life were spent in failing health (Pareto suffered from heart disease) doing some writing designed to clarify this tome. Vilfredo Federico Damaso Pareto died on August 19, 1923.

The Man: A Psychological Profile

One runs a great risk by trying to write a psychological profile for a person who is no longer with us. And yet, it is important to have some idea of the kind of man we are studying. Without being too venturesome or assertive, it is possible to identify certain qualities of character we can be reasonably sure Pareto possessed. First among these qualities was confidence in his own intellectual ability. He spent his life mastering difficult subjects and always seemed self-assured of success. It is for this reason that Pareto may, at times, have seemed to some people to be argumentative or abrasive. Ever confident of his own position, he was capable of being tenaciously steadfast on intellectual matters. This sense of confidence in his own abilities lasted until the end of his life, when he labored on the most difficult enterprise ever undertaken by a scholar, the construction of a theory of society itself. But as a result of his self-confidence, Pareto tended to be rather intolerant of persons holding opinions other than his own. He was quite capable of being terse with opponents. And his writings frequently digress into pedantic rambling.

He was at the time very egotistical and extremely sensitive to criticism.

A second prominent quality was most certainly love of freedom. We see this expressed in many ways. Pareto was, to begin with, an early champion of the oppressed in Italy.[6] He was also an ardent opponent of militarism and colonialism. Pareto was, after all, one of the few public opinion leaders of his time to speak out against Italy's 1911 war with Turkey, subsequent efforts at the "pacification" of Libya, and participation in the mayhem of the First World War. Always pitted against established political forces, Pareto was an ardent advocate of both academic freedom and free speech. And he supported his views with action. For many years Pareto offered money, shelter, and counsel to political exiles (especially in 1898 following the tumultuous events of that year in Italy). Like his father, Pareto was conservative in his personal tastes and inclinations, but he was also capable of sympathizing with others and appreciating protests for equality of opportunity and freedom of expression. Pareto was a free thinker. In some respects, he is reminiscent of an early libertarian. He was possessed of that duality of mood we continue to find among people who are extremely conservative and yet ardent in their belief in personal liberty.

It is within the realm of possibility that Pareto's love of liberty was ultimately derived from a loathing of being dominated and from an extreme need for personal autonomy. Pareto disliked being supervised by or taking orders from others, and his career experience shows steady progress in escaping from the clutches of other peoples' authority. He left his post as a government engineer for a managerial position that gave him as much autonomy as an employee can have. He eventually resigned this position in favor of self-employment as a consultant. But his income as a consultant was never assured, and he lived in a constraining environment where his political activities were watched and kept in check. Both of these problems were alleviated by leaving Italy for an academic position in Switzerland. And once Pareto became independently wealthy, he was able to chart a completely autonomous course and defy the prevailing climate of academic opinion by trying to subsume economics within the framework of his "general sociology."

Pareto's love of freedom seems also to have been associated with his hatred of bullies. With pen in hand, Pareto was clear in his denunciation of violence and oppression. He spoke out against exploitation of peasants in southern Italy and against the European military and colonial conquests of Asia and Africa. Always evenhanded and true to his principles, Pareto also spoke out against the union movement when, around 1900, some workers began to adopt violent methods and tried to justify the use of those tactics with humanitarian rhetoric. And it should be noted that Pareto's displays of bravado were not limited to quill and ink. He continued in his own political activities even under physical threat. Proficient with a sword and a fine shot with a pistol (he was fond of shooting field mice with a small caliber handgun), Pareto met intimidating threats directly and forcefully. He did not have the disposition to be kowtowed into timidity by bullies and hooligans. He was a man compelled by a deep sense of honor.

Pareto was known for his quick wit, satire, and jest. But he was also an individual disillusioned with other people. This made him somewhat cynical and gave him an air of reproach many people did not like. He was a man quick to perceive fault and unhesitant to speak out against hypocrisy. As a result, Pareto was constantly on the attack against isms from all points on the ideological spectrum: humanitarianism, liberalism, the blind optimism that comes from faith in progress, anti-semitism, nationalism, colonialism, imperialism, militarism, oligarchism, clericalism, atheism, socialism, bourgeois capitalism, unionism, syndicalism, feudalism, fascism, communism, democracy, sexism, and feminism. They were all targets of his wit and objects of his cynicism. Willing to attack anyone, Pareto was loved by few and denigrated by many. It is at least partly for this reason that his work was often rejected out of hand by people, including those who never bothered to read it. This was a great source of sorrow for Pareto, as he was confident he had unlocked some of the secrets of the social universe, and he was almost as sure that no one in his own time would recognize the enormity of his contribution.

Vilfredo Pareto was a man with a compelling sense of obligation. He was willing to be true to his principles even at great personal cost. He was a man of his word, and when he made a promise he kept it. Like many people who are deeply principled and ruled by a sense of personal obligation, Pareto was often disappointed and helplessly angered by the actions of others.

Pareto also suffered from insomnia. This is one reason he was able to become so accomplished and productive. Reading late into the night became habitual. Charming and resourceful, knowledgeable and blessed with an analytical mind, conceited with a quick wit, empathetic but incurably cynical, disillusioned yet governed by a strict code of ethics, a modest consumer but capable of appreciating the finer things in life— such was Vilfredo Pareto.

RECURRENT THEMES

Family background, life experience, and personal disposition left Pareto with certain concerns that permeated and gave direction to his work. As a consequence, a number of themes reappear in a variety of forms at various points in his career. These themes and concerns are worth noting as an important part of the historical and psychological profile of this great thinker.

Elitist Orientation

Vilfredo Pareto's ancestors were traders and merchants in and around the city of Genoa. At that time, Genoa was an important commercial and naval power, exerting some control over major shipping lanes by maintaining a series of opportune political alliances and military fortifications at strategic points such as the Bosporus Straits. Genoa profited, and her merchants and traders were the principal recipients of that prosperity. Opportunity abounded and culture flourished. This was Vilfredo Pareto's distant heritage. Even when Genoa fell on hard times, the city somehow managed to retain some semblance of its past glory by carefully managing relations with the emergent superpowers of the era: France and Austria-Hungary Vilfredo Pareto's ancestors were among the successful, and Giovanni Lorenzo Bartolomeo Pareto was ennobled with the hereditary title of Marquis during this period.

It is important not to lose sight of Pareto's mercantile and aristocratic background. He enjoyed substantial material and educational advantages all of his life. And because he suffered from insomnia, he never stopped reading or learning. Pareto's knowledge extended across the various fields of science, history, and philosophy. After finishing school, for example, he learned Greek and Latin so that he might read the classics in their original. And he was a mathematician of notable accomplishment, coming to be known, among other things, as "the father of mathematical economics."

When we consider Pareto's background, it is not surprising that he was of the old school and had a healthy regard for studied expertise and thoughtful action. Nor is it surprising that he had an equal disdain for ignorance and lack of cultivation among those claiming to be part of the intelligentsia. Pareto had compassion, even respect, for common people who in most societies are deprived of any real opportunity by accident of birth. But he loathed ignorance and hypocrisy on the part of members of an advantaged elite who have no excuse for their shortcomings and inadequacy. This may strike some readers as a self-serving elitist mentality. Others may regard it as an obvious truism. In either case, Pareto was always concerned with excellence and convinced that he was one of the few people possessed of it.

Egalitarian Meritocracy

To say that Pareto was an elitist is not to say that he favored aristocratic rule. Pareto's immediate ancestors were radicals in their own right, because they recognized the importance of having channels of mobility into the elite open to the best, brightest, and hardest working of a nation's citizenry. Their republican thinking pitted them directly against the monarchy and made them the subversive elements of their times.

Republican sentiment probably led Pareto's family to assist France during the Napoleonic period. Giovanni Benedetto Pareto (Vilfredo's grandfather, 1768-1831) was a Senator of the Republic of Genoa and a member of the Legislative Council by order of Napoleon (as well as Mayor of Genoa in 1828). Giovanni Agostino Pareto (Vilfredo's grand uncle, 1773-1820) was Minister of Finance (1800-1802) in the Napoleonic Republic of Liguria and was nominated by Napoleon to be standard-bearer.

In the next generation, Pareto's father and uncles were active supporters of Giuseppe Mazzini (a contemporary of theirs born in Genoa in 1805) and his campaign to establish an Italian republic. Mazzini organized a serious political challenge to the House of Savoy, which then ruled Genoa, having been ceded the city after the defeat of Napoleon. Needless to say, the monarchy had little appreciation for Mazzini's activities. Pareto's uncle, Damaso (1801-1862), and second cousin, Ernesto (1819-1893), were imprisoned for participation in the movement. Mazzini escaped into exile in 1834, having been saved from arrest by an aunt of Pareto's (a woman of Irish extraction) who sewed the insurgent into a mattress during a police search.

Pareto's own father, the Marquis Raffaele Pareto, followed Mazzini into exile, and he remained in France for approximately two decades. During the period of Raffaele's exile, one of his brothers was involved in clandestine activities that eventually forced King Charles Albert to grant constitutional reforms. Meanwhile, Raffaele's brother, Domenico (1804-1898), had become an important member of the establishment and served in the Piedmont government. (This is the brother of Raffaele, later to become an ambassador to the Ottoman Empire, who bequeathed a small fortune to Vilfredo Pareto in 1898.) It was while in exile in Paris that Raffaele married Marie Mattenier (1816-1889), who gave birth to Vilfredo Frederico Damasco Pareto on July 15, 1848. Pareto's two sisters were also born in Paris during this period of exile.

A Republican inclination finds recurrent expression in Pareto's work. Throughout his life he was consistently opposed to monarchy, suspicious of elites, and incensed by political rhetoric. He maintained that groups of people in political control exercise the power at their disposal in order to bolster their own positions. This inevitably means blocking the upward mobility of the most capable and energetic representatives of subordinate groups. This weakens the elite, broadens the gulf between subordinate and superordinate sectors of the population, creates a large gap between actual and potential national performance, and creates a natural reservoir of leadership for any populist movement.

Vilfredo Pareto was a man who acted on his egalitarian principles. He refused to allow others to refer to him by his hereditary title of Marquis for he truly loathed governance by a decadent aristocracy. Instead, he asked that people refer to him by achieved rather than ascribed position, as Professor Pareto.

Newtonian Vision

Vilfredo Pareto received a classical education. He was trained in the Cartesian philosophy of universal doubt and well versed in science, mathematics, literature, and history. His was an age when the prospects for scientific advancement seemed limitless and when people were convinced that systematic investigation could reveal the secrets of the universe. Indeed, this was a period when people were captivated by the Newtonian vision that the seeming chaos of the universe is reducible to, and understandable in terms of, a limited number of discrete and discoverable scientific laws.

In Pareto's estimation, Sir Issac Newton was the greatest human being who had ever lived. The Newtonian inspiration behind Pareto's work is clearly visible as early as 1869. In his college baccalaureate dissertation (1869), Pareto sets out to formalize the laws of expansion and contraction affecting all matter. This same thirst for laws is at the core of his contribution as an economist. Pareto was convinced that it would be possible to develop a science of the *social* universe and that economics was the most tangible and therefore most logical place to start. Moving beyond Maffeo Pantaleoni's pathbreaking *Pure Economics* (1889), Pareto went on to formalize and extend Leon Walrus's theory of economic equilibrium. This is a penetrating description of the interrelated nature of economic phenomena based on marginal utility and supply and demand functions.[7]

This positivistic zeal continued throughout his life and was the inspiration behind his labor-intensive investigations into sociology. Pareto summed it up nicely at the celebration of his Jubilee at Lausanne.[8] "The principal end of my studies has been to apply to the social sciences, of which economics is only a part, the experimental method which has given such brilliant results in the natural sciences." Unfortunately, Pareto was never able to capture clearly or definitively the principles of sociology for which he so ardently searched. But he did provide all the ingredients (though somewhat confused) in his *Treatise on General Sociology* (1916).[9] At least one disciple's version of his theory has been articulated in a set of succinct interrelated propositions[10] and simultaneous equations[11] of the kind Pareto would appreciate.

The Concept of Equilibrium

Pareto's concern for scientific laws left him with an avid appreciation for the importance of equilibrium dynamics. He viewed the world much as Newton did, in systemic terms. If the universe is really a complex system of interrelated parts, then dynamic forces influencing one set of components will produce change throughout the entire system. The current state of any given system can therefore be viewed as a temporary balance or moving equilibrium among dynamic forces that are subject to constant change.[12]

In his baccalaureate dissertation, Pareto attempted to account for variation in the volume of space taken up by matter. He treated expansion and contraction as countervailing forces always at work and volume as the temporary state representing an existing equilibrium or balance among those forces. Change in the overall balance or equilibrium comes about because systems are composed of interrelated parts. Whenever any component of the system is affected (by external exigencies, for example) the overall balance among countervailing forces is influenced and the character of the system changes. Thus,

Pareto used the concept of equilibrium specifically for the purpose of studying change. Any equation of Pareto's notion of equilibrium with unchanging static states (as some people are inclined to do) is misleading and erroneous.

Pareto adopted the same analytical approach in all of his later work. His economic contribution began with a successful effort to generate equations governing Walrus's theory of economic equilibrium. His efforts were then extended into the domains of power and sentiment, as Pareto sought to identify the sociopolitical forces exerting influence over (as well as being influenced by) economic events. It was to this goal that Pareto dedicated the balance of his life.

Disaffected Liberalism

In many ways, Pareto can be best understood as a disaffected liberal. An ardent republican and a constant opponent of monarchy and dictatorship early in his life, Pareto eventually lost all confidence in the will or ability of the people to recognize the truth, elect concerned leaders, or support policies designed to maximize the long-term collective good.

Vilfredo Pareto gained local acclaim with influentials in Florence after presenting a paper on "Proportional Representation" to the Academy of Geography in 1872. From that point on, he was welcome among the intellectuals and free thinkers of the community, and he frequented the Adam Smith Society, which met in the house of the renowned hostess Emilia Toscanelli-Peruzzi.[13] Developing a fervent belief in free trade, he arrived at a conclusion that was to mark an important stage in his development as a sociologist. Pareto came to understand that powerful people who favor protectionism for personal gain nevertheless always claim to be acting in the best national interest. This an assessment that was to remain with him throughout his life and flavor all of his work. Rulers use rhetoric in order to disguise their own greedy adventures.

Pareto was vocal and rather eloquent. He gathered what seemed to be a substantial following and ran for Parliament in 1881. It was at this time that Pareto had his first real taste of defeat. His loss produced bitter personal disappointment, as Pareto felt he was denied sufficient support from certain friends and notables. But more important, the results of the campaign convinced Pareto that people only hear what they want to hear. They will ignore the truth whenever it might prove to be out of harmony with their short-term interests.

Another major disappointment came in the last decade of the nineteenth century and in the first decade of the twentieth century. A political activist and liberal sympathizer, Pareto harbored a steady stream of exiles, political refugees, and renegades. But he eventually came to feel that revolutionaries are at heart no different from the corrupt rulers they seek to replace. It was Pareto's experience that the leaders of protest movements tend to be greedy and self-serving demagogues hiding behind the rhetoric of democracy and humanitarianism. (His wife also abandoned him at this time, and is said by some to have run away with a socialist.) Thus, all of Pareto's youthful and optimistic liberalism gave way to the conviction that leaders, whether in power or out, are corrupt deceivers, and the masses are easily misled.

THE END OF LIFE

Jane Régis (born in 1877) entered Pareto's life shortly after Pareto was abandoned by his wife. Madame Régis remained his lifelong companion and love. She brought Pareto happiness, and they were married in the final months of life when he was at last able to procure a divorce. They lived comfortably and happily at his villa in Céligny, a picturesque village on Lake Geneva along the road from Lausanne to Geneva.

Over the years, Pareto had gradually withdrawn from public life, having grown cautious of anyone outside his circle of closest friends and confidants. He contented himself with the company of his pride of angora cats, numbering at least 18. Near the end of life, he also developed an affinity for birds and squirrels. One of the squirrels he fed apparently pined away and starved to death after Pareto's passing. Suffering from heart disease, Vilfredo Pareto died on August 19, 1923, at the age of seventy five. His body is at rest in Céligny.

Though Pareto may have been rejected by many, he is by no means to be pitied. He lived comfortably and enjoyed the company of a loving and caring mate. Among his friends, visitors, and intellectual confidants were some of the clearest thinkers and most stimulating minds of Europe, including Maffeo Pantaleoni and Georges Sorel.

Pareto's name has enjoyed great acclaim since his death and more than a few worthy scholars have dedicated a substantial portion of their careers to continuing the memory of Pareto and extending Pareto's work. Lawrence Henderson, the famed Harvard physiologist, introduced Pareto to American scholars in the 1930s.[14] From that exposure, George Homans and Talcott Parsons, among others, went on to further clarify and popularize Pareto's ideas. Meanwhile, Arthur Livingston spent years of labor-intensive effort to edit properly the English translation of *Treatise on General Sociology* (first published in English as *The Mind and Society*). More recently, Giovanni Busino in Switzerland (as editor of *Cahiers Vilfredo Pareto*), Joseph Lopreato in the United States, and S. F. Finer in Britain have been instrumental in keeping the interest in Pareto alive. And a host of scholars have done a great deal to extend and advance Pareto's ideas. There are, to name only a few, Robert K. Merton, Crane Brinton, Juergen Backhaus, Brigette Berger, Norberto Bobbio, Warren Samuels, and Suzanne Vromen. Many others are no doubt worthy of inclusion on this list as well. All the scholarly activity surrounding Pareto's work is the best testimony of Pareto's greatness.

LIFE IN PERSPECTIVE

Pareto has occasionally been identified with the fascist movement in Europe. This identification stems chiefly from the fact that Benito Mussolini, having once been in exile at Lausanne and having apparently attended some of Pareto's classes, was fond of referring to Pareto as "the Karl Marx of the bourgeoisie." This may in itself be an appropriate label, as Pareto described societal dynamics that are thought to produce economic decline when freedom is impinged and the performance of open markets are restricted. But this is not the same as being a fascist. As Livingston notes, Pareto vehemently rejected demagogues and state tyranny.[15] Pareto was no fascist or autocract. He was, rather, a social scientist and, as S. E. Finer has described, something of a disaffected liberal.[16] Pareto was attacked by many of his contemporaries. But this may well have been because he saw error and hypocrisy for what it was. Speaking his mind on important issues, Pareto, being a natural critic, accumulated enemies from every point on the political spectrum.

NOTES

1. This chapter rests heavily on my previously published works, especially: Charles Powers, "The Life and Times of Vilfredo Pareto," in Vilfredo Pareto, *The Transformation*

of Democracy, ed. Charles Powers (R. Girola, trans.). (New Brunswick, NJ: Transaction Books, 1984). Biographical material has been collected from a number of sources. They are listed alphabetically. (1) Norberto Bobbio, *On Mosca and Pareto* (Geneva: Librairie Droz, 1972). (2) Placido Bucolo, *The Other Pareto* (New York: St. Martin's Press, 1980). (3) Giovanni Busino (ed.), *Correspondance 1890-1923*, 2 vols., (Geneva: Librairie Droz, 1975). (4) S. E. Finer, "Pareto and Pluto-Democracy: The Retreat to Galapagos," *American Political Science Review* 62 (1968). (4) Arthur Livingston, "Vilfredo Pareto: A Biographical Portrait," *Saturday Review* 12 (May 25, 1935a). (6) Arthur Livingston, "Bibliographic Note," in Vilfredo Pareto, *The Mind and Society*, ed. Arthur Livingston (A. Bongiorno and A. Livingston with J. H. Rogers, trans.) (New York: Harcourt Brace Jovanovich, 1935); reprinted by Dover in 1963 and AMS in 1983 under the original 1916 title, *Treatise on General Sociology* (after this, all citations to *Mind and Society* will be referred to as *Treatise*). (7) Maffeo Pantaleoni, "Vilfredo Pareto," *Economic Journal* 33 (September 1923): 582-590. (8) Vilfredo Pareto, "The Parliamentary Regime in Italy," *Political Science Quarterly* (1893): 677-721; reprinted in Vilfredo Pareto, *The Ruling Class in Italy before 1900* (New York: S. F. Vanni, 1950). (9) Vilfredo Pareto, *Le Mythe Vertuiste et la Littérature Immorale*, (Paris: M. Rivière, 1911). (10) Gabriele De Rosa (ed.), *Lettere a Maffeo Pantaleoni* (Rome, 1960). (11) Joseph Schumpeter, "Vilfredo Pareto, 1848-1923," *The Quarterly Journal of Economics* 63 (May 1949): 147- 173. (12), Guido Sensine, *Corrispondenza di Vilfredo Pareto* (Padua: Cedam, 1948). (13) Vincent Tarascio, *Pareto's Methodological Approach to Economics* (Chapel Hill: University of North Carolina Press, 1966).

2. Giuseppe Mazzini was forced into exile in 1834. Raffaele Pareto seems to have resided in Paris starting in 1836.

3. Dina Bakunin was apparently related to Mikhail Aleksandrovich Bakunin (1814-1876), the Russian agitator and anarchist theoretician.

4. Some sources suggest that Pareto gave up this job to work as a private consultant in 1882. It seems more likely that he left Societá Ferriere in 1889.

5. For an interesting selection of essays, see Vilfredo Pareto, *La Liberte économique et les événements d'Italie* (New York: Burt Franklin, 1968).

6. Pareto, *Parliamentary Regime*.

7. For example, see Vilfredo Pareto, *Cours d'économie politique* (Geneva: Librairie Droz, 1964), originally published 1896-1897; and Vilfredo Pareto, *Manual of Political Economy*, eds. Ann Schwier and Alfred Page (A. Schwier, trans.) (New York: August M. Kelley, 1971); translated from the second edition, which originally appeared in 1909.

8. Bernard De Voto, "Sentiment and the Social Order," *Harper's Monthly Magazine* 167 (October 1933): 569-581.

9. Pareto, *Treatise*.

10. Charles Powers, "Pareto's Theory of Society,"*Revue européenne des science sociales et cahiers Vilfredo Pareto 19* (1981) 59: 99-119.

11. Charles Powers and Robert Hanneman, "Pareto's Theory of Social and Economic Cycles: A Formal Model and Simulation," *Sociological Theory* 1 (1983): 59-89.

12. See, for example, Jean-Martin Rabot, "Le Concept D'Équilibre et la philosophie de Vilfredo Pareto," *Revue européenne des science sociales et cahiers Vilfredo Pareto 22* (1984) 67: 117-126.

13. This was an important period of intellectual growth for Pareto. He mastered Greek and Latin, immersed himself in literature, and devoured material on the history of classical civilizations.

14. Barbara Heyl, "The Harvard 'Pareto Circle'," *Journal of the History of the Behavioral Sciences* 4 (1968): 316-334. For an overall review of Pareto's impact in America, see Joseph Lopreato and Sandra Rusher, "Vilfredo Pareto's Influence on USA Sociology," *Cahiers Vilfredo Pareto* 21 (1983) 65: 69-122.

15. Livingston, *Vilfredo Pareto*.

16. Finer, *Pareto and Pluto-Democracy*.

2

Pareto's Writings
A Brief Overview

This is a book about Vilfredo Pareto's sociological theories. It was in 1898 that Pareto taught the first sociology course ever offered at Lausanne. It was not until 1901 that Pareto's first explicitly sociological essay was published, and his massive tome on sociology did not appear until 1916. So Pareto came to sociology rather late in life (after age 50) and only after accomplishing a great deal in a number of other intellectual pursuits.

Career history is of great importance. Pareto's sociology is highly distinctive because of the questions he raised and the conceptual framework he employed, both of which were cast long before he developed an interest in sociology. So it would be a mistake to analyze Pareto's sociological theories without paying some attention to his earlier work.

Pareto began his working life as an engineer and eventually joined the ranks of management. He was successful and well suited to these pursuits. He apparently enjoyed performance evaluation, systems management, and devising ways to increase output. But engineering concerns did not provide him with enough challenge. He saw that the most difficult things to understand dealt with people rather than raw material or technology, and he became enthralled with the study of history and political economy.

As his preoccupation with the social universe grew, he diverted increasing amounts of energy away from engineering or corporate endeavors, and toward political commentary. This was a period of intense intellectual struggle for Pareto. He was trying to decide what the most basic societal properties are and how social systems function. This was a great period of maturation; a transitional stage he had to traverse before being able to study the social world the way a scientist or an engineer would investigate physical properties and processes.

Although prolific and widely recognized for his commentary, it took time before Pareto came to understand societal processes in terms of equilibration and balance among countervailing forces. Interaction between supply and demand provided him with a clear framework for his analysis, and it was here that Pareto began to build his science of society. His accomplishments in this regard were seminal, and by early in the twentieth century he was widely regarded as "the father of mathematical economics."

But Pareto found a conservative approach to economics to be disappointing. He was convinced that the most important questions about economic performance are affected by sociopolitical factors and can only be answered by studying the social and political contexts in which economic events occur. It was at this point that Pareto began thinking about society as a holistic system and then began writing his sociological essays.

Pareto's sociological theories can only be properly understood if one keeps his earlier works in mind. As a scientifically inclined engineer, Pareto viewed phenomena in terms of shifting balance among counter-vailing forces in complex systems composed of interrelated parts. As a commentator, Pareto identified the important properties that, in varying degrees, characterize every society. Productivity, inequality, and social mobility are examples. As an economist, Pareto tried to account for temporal change in economic conditions: the business cycle. But the economy is not autonomous and business cycles do not operate in vacuums. The "system," properly identified, is the society as a whole, and economies are embedded within societies. Hence, Pareto's sociology evolved directly out of his earlier work as an engineer, manager, commentator, and economist.

Pareto's works, especially his sociological works, are often elusive and obtuse. So recognizing the continuity in his various writings makes it easier to appreciate the real intent and power of his sociological theories. This chapter provides a brief summary of the contributions he made over the course of his career, and thus sets the stage for more detailed treatment of his sociological theories in the chapters to follow.[1]

PARETO AS AN ENGINEER AND MANAGER (1865-1888)

Pareto received a solid education, culminating with professional training at the Polytechnic Institute of Turin, Italy. His baccalaureate dissertation (1869) is more than a student paper written to fulfill a requirement. It is a clear statement of the philosophy of science Pareto would continue to apply throughout his life. As such, it deserves special attention.

The goal of Pareto's thesis was to present an integrated package of equations defining elasticity in solids ("Fundamental Principles of the Theory of Elasticity in Solid Bodies and Research Concerning the Integration of Differential Equations Defining Their Equilibrium"). In this essay, every solid is viewed as a system composed of interdependent parts. By virtue of this interdependence, anything that influences any set of components (for instance, the application of heat) has consequences for other components in the system. These consequences spread via the operation of countervailing forces of attraction and repulsion. Scientists try to explain the operation of these forces in terms of a limited number of principles. Given these internal dynamics, balance will tend to stabilize around certain equilibrium points (e.g., a given volume) if the system remains relatively undisturbed by outside shocks. But external shocks (such as the application of more heat) stimulate the operation of internal dynamics, and this can result in re-equilibration (expansion or contraction) at a different system state (volume).[2]

This approach to science has several important features. (1) To begin with, a clear distinction is made between the dynamic processes that are internal to a system and shocks from the external environment that may trigger those processes. (2) It is assumed that systems are composed of generic properties that can be identified. (3) The operation of countervailing forces can either stimulate or impede change, depending on specific empirical conditions, so the same theoretical framework can be used to study both stability and change. (4) Change in one system component results in predictable modifications throughout the system because of mutual interdependence among elements. And (5) change in one direction can stimulate countervailing forces that resist further movement in the same direction.

As employed by Pareto, the concept of equilibrium does not imply that existing systems are good. Nor does it imply that the world is static. All equilibria experience change because internal adjustments are made as the elements of a system are affected by external exigencies, and this happens constantly unless a system is in a complete vacuum. Given that change is constant, the goal of science should not be to describe any static state. The goal of science, according to Pareto, should be to reveal the operation of countervailing processes that produce internal structural alterations when a system is subjected to external stimuli.

Later stages in Pareto's work can be viewed as a slow process of clarifying concepts and discovering principles that would enable him to apply his equilibrium perspective in the analysis of social systems. As his work progressed, Pareto constructed social theory as similar to theory in the physical sciences as he could make it.

Pareto's first opportunity to apply his scientific perspective to the social world came when he assumed management responsibilities at Societá Ferriere Italiana. It was in this position that he gained a full grasp of the complexities of an industrial corporation. The practical problems he had to deal with included transit of freight, shifting exchange rates, customs duties in the case of foreign trade, and labor problems, in addition to the technical factors involved in production. Ever conceptualizing the world in systemic terms, he found it useful to identify the major system properties and processes he had to deal with, and to keep their interrelated nature clearly in mind. He gained great practical knowledge that was to prove very useful later.

At the same time, Pareto began to develop an interest in political commentary. He was invited to contribute to the Bulletin of the Academy of Geography after presenting a particularly well-received paper on "Proportional Representation" to the Academy on June 29, 1872. And Pareto was a vocal member of the Adam Smith Society and contributer to its newsletter. Pareto was a radical (free trade) candidate for parliament in 1882 but was rejected by the voters. It was not until 1889 that he really launched into his endeavors as a political commentator with the full energy of a Titan.

PARETO AS A POLITICAL COMMENTATOR (1889-1893)

The year 1889 marked a substantial change in life course for Pareto. His mother (Marie Mattenier, 1816-1889) died that year. He married

Dina Bakunin, gave up his engineering position for life as a consultant, moved to Villa Rosa in Frisole, and began writing commentaries and reviews at a fever pitch. Approximately 160 of his items were published over a four-year period. It seems clear that Pareto was ready for a new challenge.

Pareto understood what the goals and methods of science should be, but in the 1880's the social sciences were as yet undeveloped. It is not surprising, therefore, that when Pareto began publishing his thoughts on current events, the resulting articles took the form of insightful and informed journalism rather than social science as it would eventually come to be practiced. And yet, this stage in life was crucial to Pareto's development as a sociologist. Without a well-developed social scientific foundation laid by others, Pareto had to discover for himself what the important features of the social world are. Pareto's penetrating insight and the distinctly modern nature of his political criticism reflect a sophisticated understanding of social phenomena and relationships among structural components of social systems. Focusing on interests, beliefs, power, classes, mobility, social control, and social change, the basic elements of Pareto's sociology are all present, in embryonic form, in his commentary.

Most of Pareto's articles are polemic statements aimed at influencing public policy. Because Pareto was a strict advocate of free trade, open competition, and freedom from government intervention, his commentary is designed to convince readers that protective tariffs and other forms of government involvement in the economy tend to undermine the general prosperity.[3] Governments err by passing tariffs, granting monopoly rights to large corporations, erecting barriers against entry of new firms into the market, and insulating some companies with subsidies, purchases, and loans. These measures tend to support uneconomical endeavors that might otherwise fail, thus freeing resources that could be more productively used elsewhere. At the same time, obstacles to the establishment and survival of new firms protect large corporations from indigenous competition, limit avenues of mobility, and enable existing companies to raise prices inordinately causing a transfer of wealth from working people to the rich. Given that giant corporations rather than struggling entrepreneurs are most likely to receive government protection, the "need to assist foundling industries" must be viewed as a mistruth designed to generate public acceptance of undesirable practices.

Pareto was also a vocal opponent of militarization and colonial expansion. Far from being in the national interest, he saw Italian occupation of African territories as a wasteful diversion of funds away from meaningful capital investment. In his opinion, it would have been far wiser to build factories or house people than to make cannons or burn gunpowder. In the final analysis, colonial adventure profits the rich at the expense of the working people who bear a disproportionate share of the costs for such government operations. But few people recognize this. Politicians are always adept at justifying pillage and plunder overseas in the name of lofty moral causes or perceived national interest.

Pareto was perplexed by the longevity of exploitive governments and lying politicians. Turning his attention away from the mechanisms of exploitation and to the topic of political survival, he focused on the importance of co-optation. Corrupt regimes are able to resist change because the zeal for reform decays quickly among those who profit, even in small ways, from the system. Most people support existing institutions for the sole reason that those institutions do dispense some benefits. Overt repression of dissidents is seldom necessary, at least in industrial societies that have socioeconomic ladders with many tiers, because most people devote their attention to making small personal gains and can be easily and rather inexpensively co-opted.

However, the dynamics of social control are different in peasant societies. Exploitation is more visible because there is a wider socioeconomic rift between the dominant and subordinate classes, and because each class is internally more homogeneous. In Naples, where class differences were large and exploitation overt at the time Pareto was writing, hostility against the bourgeoisie ran high and the people were brutally suppressed. Any relaxation of the suppression simply allowed the existing hostility to find new expression in revolt or subversive activity.[4]

Pareto's commentary reflects his emerging analytical style and his clear effort to debunk existing ideologies; an effort for which he was harassed by the authorities. Many propositions can be derived from the commentary. For instance, the more structurally differentiated a community is, then the less likely members of subordinate classes are to be unified by class consciousness. By 1893, Pareto had a sharpened awareness of social structure and process, but he remained uncertain how to combine these insights into a scientific theory. He found himself attracted to the study of economics because economists were dealing with relatively tangible phenomena and were beginning to articulate some abstract theoretical principles.

PARETO AS AN ECONOMIST (1891-1909)

Pareto's tenure as an academically oriented economist can probably be dated from 1891. It was in that year that Pareto, after reading Maffeo Pantaleoni's *Pure Economics* (1889),[5] became convinced that social science was really possible and that economics would be the first of the social sciences to advance. Pantaleoni was much impressed when Pareto extended the general principles that were advanced in *Pure Economics*. He encouraged Pareto to reread the works of Leon Walrus and try to formalize Walrus's theory of economic equilibrium. And it was on Pantaleoni's suggestion that Walrus, who was then retiring from his post as Professor of Political Economy at the University of Lausanne, recommended that he be replaced by Vilfredo Pareto. This was a well-timed offer of employment, for Pareto was coming under increasing pressure for his political activities and had decided it was time to leave Italy.

Once at Lausanne, Pareto set about clarifying and mathematically defining Walrus's theory of economic equilibrium much as he had done for the theory of molecular mechanics in his baccalaureate thesis. Pareto remained true to this objective and always gave Walrus his justly deserved credit, although the personalities of the two men did not mesh and there was some acrimony between them.

Pareto's *Course in Political Economy* (1896-97) was a direct product of teaching Walrus's economics class.[6] This work was largely a clarification and extension of Walrus's ideas but also established Pareto's reputation as an economist of note. *Course* was an attempt to develop economics as a formal discipline organized under the rubric of general equilibrium theory. It is a description of the interrelated nature of economic phenomena stressing mutual dependence of elements in the same system.

Pareto proceeded from a unified equilibrium framework to investigate major economic functions involved in production. Yet, although *Course* is a pioneering work in the formalization of economics, Pareto's arguments continued to be influenced by free trade and laissez-faire polemics. In many ways, *Course* is a defense of classical economics and an attempt to demonstrate mathematically the position that tariffs destroy national wealth.[7]

Course is also noteworthy for Pareto's treatment of motivation. Unlike many of his contemporaries, Pareto followed Adam Smith and Herbert Spencer in rejecting the notion that human behavior is rational. He argued that those who believe that people behave logically are apt to develop misleading theories. People may logically seek to maximize the realization of certain goals, but why people select certain goals and priorities is beyond the domain of logic.

Pareto also introduced his "law of income distribution" in *Course*,[8] and developed it more thoroughly in later articles.[9] He contended that wealth is more or less normally distributed with a constant income differential between "the haves and have nots" in any society. Although nonrevolutionary political reform may result in minor vacillations in inequality, or in the development of different mechanisms of exploitation, it is unlikely to result in drastic or permanent reductions in relative inequality because those in power always try to protect their own interests and privileges. The rich and powerful cannot realistically be expected to implement programs seriously designed to eliminate inequality. This has an important policy implication. Assuming that the relative shares of the "economic pie" accruing to different social classes remains essentially constant, reform measures are unlikely to have much impact on stratification. Therefore, the best way to reduce poverty is to "bake a bigger pie" by increasing productivity. Pareto's law of income distribution was a highly original contribution and generated a whole field of research literature in economics (public welfare policy). It is, in that sense, one of his major accomplishments.

Pareto's interests began to move in other directions after 1898 when he taught his first sociology course. But he continued to make important contributions as an economist. The first edition of *Manual of Political Economy* was published in 1906 just before his retirement. A substantially revised version was published in 1909.[10] This revised version, his first project after retirement, was a highly important work long regarded by economists as a true classic. The appendix to the 1909 edition is of particular importance, for it is here that Pareto presents a system of equations formalizing and integrating economic theory more effectively than had been done elsewhere up to that point.

Pareto regarded *Manual of Political Economy* as his final contribution to an emergent science. In it he rejects his past polemics and makes a sustained effort to limit the intrusion of his own values. And an examination of his conceptual framework will prove useful. Pareto envisioned most economic functions as balanced compromises between *tastes*—desires that people wish to satisfy—and *obstacles*—those factors that prevent or impede the satisfaction of tastes. Logic may have nothing to do with determination of tastes, but once tastes develop, individuals are assumed to make logical choices calculated to maximize *ophelimity*—a neutral term for utility or the satisfaction of tastes—in light of known obstacles. Aggregate patterns of economic behavior (e.g., propensity to save versus conspicuous consumption) constitute very useful data because they indicate what trade-offs people are making as they try to maximize ophelimity.

Demand provides a clear example of the shifting balance between tastes and obstacles. Advertising can stimulate the taste people have for some products while dampening the taste for others. People convinced by advertising that they must buy one product are simultaneously convinced, even if only by stealth, to avoid possible substitutes. But demand is more than a function of tastes. It is also a function of obstacles. High prices, lack of availability, illegality, and other obstacles can all operate to dampen demand even if people hunger for the items concerned.

The balance between tastes and obstacles is an extremely useful analytical tool because it can be used to conceptualize most economic functions. For example, the desire (taste) to produce goods and services is based primarily upon profit potential. But products offering the greatest profit potential (e.g., cars) often involve the greatest obstacles to production. Despite the prospects for substantial profit, few firms engage in heavy industry because few can mobilize the resources necessary to overcome obstacles to production.

This conceptual framework is made more useful by the fact that the balance among tastes and obstacles for one economic function is inextricably linked with the balance among tastes and obstacles for other economic functions. For instance, increased obstacles to production raise the price necessary to encourage firms to supply commodities, and those price increases tend to dampen demand and thus reduce overall profit potential. Both functions, supply and demand, are part of a single system of interdependence operating on the basis of general principles. Price is a structural elaboration of that system. A change in any major component of the system (for example: wages, cost of raw materials, market size, technology, adequacy of transportation) will result in adjustments throughout the system, and those adjustments are predictable. Other major components of the economic system can also be viewed as structural elaborations generated by equilibrium dynamics. These include capital formation, investment, number of firms, size of firms, employment, and inflation rate.[11]

Two kinds of equilibrium movement can take place. *Stable equilibrium* occurs when a change in one component of a system stimulates modifications that tend to minimize or reverse the original change. For example, an increase in consumer demand can lead to price increases that ultimately dampen demand. *Unstable equilibrium* occurs when change in one component of a system results in modifications that tend to amplify the initial change. For instance, increasing demand can lead to an increase in the number of competing suppliers, changes in economy of scale, or technological innovations, each of which can result in lower prices and stimulate still greater demand.[12] The hand calculator boom of the 1970s and personal computer boom of the 1980s are excellent examples.

An important conclusion to be drawn from all this is that, although people may try to maximize fulfillment of their own objectives, there is no invisible hand guiding economic outcomes toward any optimal solutions such as the greatest good for the greatest number of citizens. So changes that work to the advantage of some may well work to the disadvantage of others and whole sectors of the population can suffer as a result. Pareto pointed out that the deleterious effects of such changes can be ameliorated by transfers or support payments for the disadvantaged. This was a radical statement of opinion at the time and provided the foundation on which "welfare economics" was constructed by later economists.[13]

For Pareto, the economy constitutes an equilibrated system because:

(a) major components of the economy can be identified,
(b) a few simple principles describe the nature of interdependence among parts of the system,
(c) mutual dependence among parts requires that a change in any aspect of the system is followed by modifications throughout the system, and
(d) as a general rule, change in one direction eventually tends to generate its own forces of resistance.

The operation of these dynamics results in continual oscillation, so that it is impossible to conceive of a single economic state as being the only natural, optimal, or desirable solution for the economy to reach.

Thus, ophelimity is employed in a more sophisticated way in *Manual* than it was in *Course*.[14]

The final quarter of *Manual* reflects the mood that led Pareto to make his sociological contributions. No longer content to examine economic functions like price or supply in isolation, Pareto sought to investigate the dynamics that make societies operate as holistic socio-economic and political systems.

PARETO AS A SOCIOLOGIST (1898-1923)

The year 1898 marked another major turning point in the life of Vilfredo Pareto. His uncle Domenico Pareto died, leaving Vilfredo a small fortune and the financial independence he had always yearned for. It was in the same year that Pareto began to divert his attention away from economics and toward the fledgling science of sociology. Pareto was to make several important contributions to the advancement of economics over the next decade, but these contributions came as he brought to fruition projects that were already well under way. After 1898, any new undertakings fell squarely within the realm of sociology.

Pareto's first sociological work, "Un applicazione di teorie socio-logiche" (1901), was introduced to English-speaking audiences as *The Rise and Fall of the Elites* by Hans Zetterberg in 1968.[15] In this work, Pareto sought to identify the major features of society that fluctuate cyclically, to describe the movement of these cycles in equilibrium terms, and to indicate ways in which the structural features and general form of society emerge from the equilibrium being described.

The Rise and Fall of the Elites is the initial statement of the theory of "circulation of elites" for which Pareto was to become so well known. But in fact, there is much more in this revealing essay. It is really an outline for all of Pareto's later sociological work. The nature of political control, business activity, and popular sentiment (as reflected in religious feeling, ideology, etc.) are viewed as undulating cyclically. The goal of sociology is to understand the equilibrium dynamics that produce social change and give it a predictable character.

All of Pareto's later sociological works are based on the agenda established in *The Rise and Fall of the Elites*. *Les Systémes socialistes* (1902-03) provides a justification for sociology.[16] Pareto's one-million word tome, *Treatise on General Sociology* (1916), provides the evidence for his position.[17] And Pareto's last monograph, *The Transformation of*

Democracy (1921), restates the basic position, making certain pivotal readjustments.[18]

Pareto begins his analysis (1901) by positing that every human being is motivated by *sentiments*—subconscious beliefs that serve as standards of evaluation. What he meant by sentiment was only vaguely defined in 1901, but the intended meaning became more clear and precise in his later works (especially 1916). For sociological purposes, the most important sentiments are *combinations*—cunning, guile, and the inclination to innovate—and *persistence of aggregates*—stubborn adherence to established ways and insistence on the preservation of traditions.

Individuals are characterized by a mixture of both sentiments, but every individual tends to be dominated by one more than the other. Considering society as a whole, aggregate patterns of sentiment change over time. There are some periods when blind adherence to tradition is encouraged and other periods when conservatism is besmirched and guile and innovation rewarded. Thus, the popular sentiments that characterize a society undulate, moving through successive cycles of "faith" and "skepticism." Religions and other dogmas that do not rely on logical validation are prevalent during periods of conservative "faith." Pseudological ideologies like humanitarianism are prevalent during periods of liberal "skepticism."

The character of a society changes rather markedly as the general populace is swayed by alternating moods of skepticism and faith, somehow akin to liberalism and conservatism. But in *Elites*, Pareto pays particular attention to the sentiments dominant among political elites. Like any other group, the governing elite is composed of two kinds of people. Those dominated by the sentiment of "combinations" have cunning and guile. They prefer to rule through co-optation, diplomatic intrigue, and deviousness. Those dominated by the sentiment of "persistence of aggregates" are direct and prefer to rule through the use of unbridled force. Pareto referred to these two types of leaders as foxes and lions, respectively.

If a governing elite is going to stay in power, it must be able to defend its privileged status. It is for this reason that heterogeneity is very important. An elite composed of a balanced mix of lions and foxes will derive power from its ability to exercise control through a combination of co-optation and force ("carrot and stick" tactics). But a homogeneous elite loses power by virtue of its sole reliance on one single strategy for maintaining social control. A regime that tries to maintain itself exclusively through the use of force cannot last. Neither can a regime that bases its position entirely on co-optation.

Until very late in his life, Pareto had a habit of viewing political history as a series of changes in leadership. This placed a focus on the circulation occurring as members of subordinate classes experience upward mobility into the governing elite. Circulation progresses gradually if the group in power occasionally recruits new people with special talents. However, an elite enjoying power typically tries to buttress its position against subordinate underlings, thus restricting mobility. And the few outsiders that are recruited may have the same traits ("combinations" versus "persistences of aggregates") already present in the elite, thus resulting in further homogenization. An elite that becomes homogeneous declines in power and leaves itself open for revolutionary overthrow.

Pareto was particularly interested in what he regarded as the decline of the elite occurring in his own time. His impression was that the European elites around 1900 were strong in "combinations" and weak in "persistences of aggregates." In other words, they were crafty, deceitful, and cunning, but unable to act in a direct and forceful manner. The spread of humanitarian ideology was a symptom of their deterioration. At the time, it was popular for members of the elite to express sympathy with the downtrodden masses. And if forced to the point of confrontation, the governing classes were loathe to use force. From Pareto's point of view, this meant that any powerful group (including big business or organized labor) could act with impunity without fear of reprisal. Weakness on the part of the elite in power undermined the credibility of government. But the fatal strain came because the hypocrites in power were far less humanitarian than they professed. Making a few charitable contributions here and there, their greed nevertheless went unreined and knew no bounds. Driven by limitless desires, they profited and exploited as much as possible and incurred the jealousy and ire of everyone. Resistance to their rule rose at the same time that their ability to retain control diminished.

Pareto argued in his early sociological writings that circulation of political elites, or change from dominance by "lions" to dominance by "foxes" and back again, occurs cyclically as first one personality type and then the other dominates the elite ranks. This cyclical change is unavoidable. Every governing elite tends over time to perfect a particular strategy for domination, thus becoming homogeneous. But in becoming homogeneous, an elite group weakens itself, increasing the prospects that it will be supplanted.[19]

Economic elites circulate in much the same way. A "rentier" is a member of the economic elite in whom the sentiment of "group persistence" is strong; and a "speculator" is a member of the economic elite in whom the sentiment of combination is strong. "Speculators" tend to be successful during expansionary periods when capital is available for investment, and "rentiers" tend to be successful during periods of consolidation. But those who are successful under one set of economic conditions are unlikely to have the qualities necessary for continued success and retention of their favored positions under the changing conditions that eventually arise.

By the time Pareto wrote *Les Systémes socialistes* (1902-1903), he had become firmly and unequivocally convinced that most human behavior is motivated and guided by nonlogical considerations that are covered by a veneer of ex post facto and false logic developed in order to satisfy a human craving for the security of having acted rationally. For Pareto, this simple recognition means that explanations of behavior in terms of rationality are based on false premises and can only lead to erroneous conclusions. Hence, in Pareto's eye, a more conclusive science than economics would need to be developed if scientific understanding of society is to advance. In this sense, *Les Systémes socialistes* (1902-03) can be regarded as a justification for the sociological agenda Pareto laid out in *The Rise and Fall of the Elites* (1901). But it also provides a first glimpse of the dynamic processes causing the patterns Pareto described in 1901.

Pareto developed two basic insights in *Systémes*. First, people react to events as they are perceived within a system of beliefs rather than as they actually are. This is similar to W. I. Thomas's important recognition that "definition of situation" is nearly all important in determining human behavior. Because ideologies are based on sentiment rather than reason, they are all—in a figurative sense—forms of religion predicated on either faith or skepticism.[20] Faith is associated with accepting a dogma without demanding logical validation. Skepticism, on the other hand, tends to be associated with pseudological ideologies. Faith generally reflects the sentiment of "persistence of aggregates" and skepticism generally reflects the sentiment of "combinations," so different kinds of dogma will gain and lose popularity with undulations in public sentiment. Pareto argued that investigators err by paying attention to the doctrinal specifics of various dogmas. As far as Pareto was concerned, ideologies are only of interest as indicators of underlying sentiments.

The second theme in *Systémes* is that ideologies necessarily cycle over time. Adherence to dogmas of faith cannot be maintained because logical contradictions between dogma and reality become apparent. Adherence to dogmas of skepticism cannot be maintained because they eventually make behavioral prescriptions so equivocal that they lose their social utility. One sentiment with its corresponding ideologies is overemphasized until contradictions become apparent and a reaction in the opposite direction sets in.[21]

Les Systémes socialistes stimulated considerable controversy for the negative light in which it portrayed humanitarian and socialist movements. Pareto's sympathies seem to have changed markedly in the preceding years and he makes a number of inflammatory comments. However, Pareto's efforts should be construed as an attempt to expose the nonlogical nature of ideology more than as an effort to attack left-leaning ideologies or attract converts to his own political persuasion. Pareto's worldview was conservative in orientation. But the ultimate lesson of Pareto's sociology is that there is no right or wrong kind of social system. Every state of affairs contains strains and contradictions that make change inexorable.[22]

After retiring from the University of Lausanne in 1907, "the lone thinker of Céligny" began work on what was to be the climax of his intellectual career. Pareto's *Treatise on General Sociology* was completed in 1914, published in Italian in 1916, and translated into English for publication in 1935. The *Treatise* presents an analysis of society as a complex system of interrelated parts in equilibrium. It is in this work that the concept of social system is forcefully employed, with social, economic, and political variables bound to one another in relationships of mutual determination. A change in any aspect of the social system necessitates changes in the rest of the system, and changes in the character of social systems must be understood in terms of mutual dependence among system elements.[23]

The importance of each prior stage in the development of Pareto's thought becomes clear in *Treatise on General Sociology*. Pareto modified the equilibrium model he had adopted as an engineer by introducing the societal properties he first focused on as a political commentator and by trying to define the nature of interdependence among these properties with the same social scientific rigor that he defined interrelations among various economic functions.

Long sections of Pareto's *Treatise* are taken up with a laborious defense of the assumptions he felt necessitated the development of sociology as a new field of inquiry. First, human behavior is, for the most part, nonlogical. Therefore, it cannot be understood within the limits of economic models. Second, human behavior is motivated by rhythmically changing sentiments, and hence, cannot be viewed as either constant or as historically unique. And third, human behavior is not motivated by the forces to which people attribute their actions, and thus, it cannot be adequately understood in ideological terms or within the confines of conventional wisdom.

From Pareto's point of view, these three tenets suggested the need for a particular kind of sociology: a "general sociology." His goals were to identify the most important features of social systems and to articulate a limited number of general principles accounting for observed patterns of social change. The societal properties he identified were public sentiments, economic interests, and circulation of political elites. Each of these three components fluctuates cyclically. Furthermore, movement on one cycle tends to be correlated with movement on the others. Depending on a society's position on these coordinated cycles, a different set of structural properties will emerge. The character of each society changes as it moves along these three equilibrated cycles.

When Pareto referred to sentiment as a component in societal equilibrium, he meant that there are changes in the relative distribution of "combinations" and "persistence of aggregates" as basic drives. These sentiments shift in emphasis with the times. When skepticism prevails, humanitarian ideologies are popular, people are more willing to indulge themselves with consumer purchases, nonconformity spreads, and sexual expression is tolerated. During periods when faith is prevalent, formal religions gain in popularity, people tend to forgo unnecessary consumption in favor of saving, conformity is encouraged, and sexual expression is punished. So the flavor of a society changes quite substantially with the times. Cyclical change is inevitable because life is far from satisfactory in any society. When skepticism prevails, social prescriptions become too equivocal for people's tastes and a reaction sets in. But people object when rules come to be more constraining, and a reaction then develops in the opposite direction. Movement in one direction moves forward a considerable distance under its own momentum (as when people demand enforcement of rules). But movement continues under the force of this momentum until an extreme is reached and people clamor for a reversal of prevailing trends (as when people demand the relaxation of rules). So a pendulous cycle emerges. Yet, the operation of these dynamics tends to be obscured by the ideological covering that is ultimately applied to most events.[24]

A similar cycle occurs in the economy. Periods of growth and expansion are preceded and followed by periods of contraction and decline. A pool of savings and underutilized resources accumulates during extended periods of economic downturn. This accumulated pool of savings provides the investment capital that stimulates economic growth and expansion. But Pareto argued that expansionary periods are characterized by inflation, capital depletion, and other factors that make sustained growth impossible. So again, movement in one direction generates sources of resistance that produce a reversal of the trend, and a pattern of cyclical undulation makes itself apparent.

In *Treatise on General Sociology* (1916), Pareto repeated his earlier (1901) analysis of the circulation of elites in which lions and foxes alternately occupy leadership positions. But his psychologistic analysis is largely abandoned in favor of a more structural approach by 1921 when Pareto produced his final monograph, *The Transformation of Democracy*. By that time, the notion of circulating elites had largely given way to an analysis of centralization and decentralization of power governed by the operation of centripetal and centrifugal forces that are structural in character rather than manifestations of the personalities of individual actors.[25]

Centripetal force is generated when people clamor for stabilization of their environments, removal of uncertainty, and protection against unbridled exploitation at the hands of diverse interests acting with impunity. Under these conditions, people appreciate the benefits that central authority can provide and the power of central government grows. But central government generates its own opposition as it becomes flagrant in its exercise of raw force. Resistance builds until maintenance of highly centralized government becomes untenable and power is decentralized.

In the initial stages, decentralization brings real advantages. A wider array of interests finds that channels for meaningful political participation are opened up and the government becomes more responsive. Benefits become widely dispersed because decentralized governments tend to rule through co-optation. But when co-optation becomes blatant and widespread, a massive gap develops between actual and potential performance. Work incentive is lost. Instead, people convince themselves that benefits are distributed solely on the basis of largess without regard to quality of performance.

This was the kind of society that had, in Pareto's estimation, developed in Italy by 1920. It was a "pluto democracy." It had elements of a plutocracy because it was ruled by an oligarchic capitalist elite that made all the important decisions and, controlling events from behind the scenes, ensured itself of enormous wealth and profits. But it also had elements of a democracy. Universal franchise for men meant that some kind of power had been transferred to the masses. The capitalist elite stayed in power by adopting policies that were to the liking of national labor unions and other groups capable of delivering large blocks of votes. The people who suffered were small businessmen, nonunionized labor, and other people who lacked protection. A reaction did set in as Pareto predicted, and Benito Mussolini took power in October of 1922.

Both *Treatise on General Sociology* and *The Transformation of Democracy* emphasize the interdependent nature of the cycles of sentiment, productivity, and power. Each cycle synchronizes the others in predictable ways. For example, economic downturn and political centralization tend to discourage skeptical outlooks on life and encourage faith. As faith becomes more widespread, people consume less and save more. This has the short-term effect of constricting the economy even more by choking off consumer purchases, but it has the long-term effect of creating a reservoir of saving that can be drawn on for future investment. Linkages between the three cycles produce a socioeconomic transformation of far-reaching proportions.

PARETO'S WORK IN OVERVIEW

It is amazing how much continuity there is in the work produced at various stages of Pareto's life. He was, above all, a scientist. As an engineer he adopted a model of science based on molecular mechanics and principles of equilibration. With this model of science in mind, he strove to isolate important properties of social systems, to make empirical generalizations about how those properties change over time, and to generate abstract principles that account for those patterns of observable change.

Although trained in the natural sciences, Pareto was nonetheless always more fascinated by the social world than the physical world.

Perhaps this is because he regarded social science as the greatest and most perplexing of man's challenges. As a political observer and commentator he isolated many of the basic properties of the social universe, and as an economist he adopted equilibrium theory to the study of the most tangible and manageable of these processes. Near the end of his life, Pareto finally felt competent to accept the challenge of sociology: the development of a theory of society itself. The various elements of this theory will be reviewed in the chapters that follow.

NOTES

1. This chapter builds upon my unpublished manuscript, Charles Powers,"Pareto's Sociology" (1979, 112 pps.). This manuscript formed the basis of three book chapters on Pareto written by Charles Powers, Jonathan Turner, and Leonard Beeghley, and appearing in Jonathan Turner and Leonard Beeghley, *The Emergence of Sociological Theory* (Homewood, IL: Dorsey, 1981).

2. Vilfredo Pareto, "Principi fondamentali della teoria della elasticitá de' corpi solidi e ricerche sulla integrazione delle equazioni differenziali che ne definiscono l'equilibrio," originally published in 1869; reprinted in Vilfredo Pareto, *Scritti teorici*, ed. G. Demaria (Milan: Malfasi, 1952, pps. 593-639).

3. Vilfredo Pareto, *La Liberté économique et les événements d'Italie* (New York: Burt Franklin, 1968).

4. Vilfredo Pareto, "The Parliamentary Regime in Italy," *Political Science Quarterly* (1893, pps. 677-721); reprinted in Vilfredo Pareto, *The Ruling Class in Italy Before 1900* (New York: S. F. Vanni, 1950).

5. Maffeo Pantaleoni, *Pure Economics* (London: Macmillan, 1898); originally published in 1889.

6. Vilfredo Pareto, *Cours d'économie politique* (Geneva: Librairie Droz, 1964).

7. Ibid., sections 864ff.

8. Ibid., section 965.

9. See, for example, Vilfredo Pareto, *Escruits sur la Courbe de la Repartition de la Richesse* (Geneva: Librairie Droz, 1965).

10. Vilfredo Pareto, *Manual of Political Economy* eds. Ann Schwier and Alfred Page (A. Schwier, trans.) (New York: August M. Kelley, 1971); translated from the revised edition originally published in 1909. The first edition was published in 1906.

11. Ibid., chapter 3.

12. Vilfredo Pareto, *"L'économie mathématique,"* in *Encyclopedie des sciences mathématiques* (Paris, 1911).

13. Pareto, *Manual.* Also see Warren Samuels, *Pareto on Policy* (New York: Elsevier, 1974).

14. Pareto, *Manual.*

15. Vilfredo Pareto, *The Rise and Fall of the Elites* (introduced by Hans Zetterberg) (Totowa, NJ: Bedminster, 1968); originally published in 1901.

16. Vilfredo Pareto, *Les Systémes socialistes* (Geneva: Librairie Droz, 1965); originally published in 1902-1903.

17. Vilfredo Pareto, *Mind and Society*, ed. Arthur Livingston (A. Bongiorno and A. Livingston with J. H. Rogers, trans.) (New York: Harcourt Brace Jovanovich, 1935); reprinted by Dover in 1963 and AMS in 1983 under the original 1916 title, *Treatise on General Sociology* (hereafter, *Treatise*).

18. Vilfredo Pareto, *The Transformation of Democracy*, ed. Charles Powers (R. Girola, trans.) (New Brunswick, NJ: Transaction Books, 1984); originally published in 1921.

19. Pareto, *Elites*, pps. 30-31, 36, 40-41, 56-60, 68-70.

20. Pareto, *Les Systémes*, chapter 5.

21. Ibid., chapters 1 and 6.

22. See, for example, Vilfredo Pareto, *Le Mythe Vertuiste et la Littérature Immorale* (Paris: M. Riviére, 1911).

23. Pareto, *Treatise*.

24. Vilfredo Pareto, *Fatti e Teorie* (Florence: Vallecchi, 1920).

25. Pareto, *Transformation*.

3

Building A Science
Pareto's Views on Theory Construction

Vilfredo Pareto dedicated the latter part of his life to molding sociology into a real science. As he often expressed, "my wish is to construct a system of sociology on the model of celestial mechanics, physics, chemistry."[1] This intent is absolutely essential to keep in mind when considering his work. Readers who lose sight of Pareto's goal are likely to overlook the core of his theory. For his essays tend to be full of digressions and diatribe. It is only by seeing where Pareto is going that we are able to recognize it when he gets there.

Pareto himself clearly regarded philosophy of science as an important starting point. *Treatise on General Sociology*,[2] and also *Manual of Political Economy*,[3] both open with detailed discussions of theory construction and methodological techniques appropriate to the social sciences. Coming to grips with Pareto's approach to theory construction is therefore an important step in our effort to discover and clarify the sociological theory that rests implicitly in his work.

HOW IS SCIENCE DONE?

Pareto adopted the natural sciences for his ideal model of how science should develop. From this point of view, theory is the heart and essence of science. This follows from the fact that the ultimate goal of scientific inquiry is to generate a body of succinct but powerful laws that enable us to account for patterns of events in the universe under study.

Observing Regularities and Making Empirical Generalizations

Science proceeds, in Pareto's view, in a series of systematic steps. The first stage of scientific inquiry is to make general observations about the world around us. Empirical generalizations about the way things seem to be constitute the data scientists ponder and the patterned phenomena scientists attempt to explain.

People often never get as far as the first stage of scientific inquiry. Rather than trying to identify patterns and regularities in the world, they preoccupy themselves with definitional arguments and epistemological debates. Such debates are wholly counterproductive, for arguing about definitions or approaches only serves to prevent us from attaining our ends.[4] For example, if we were to avoid making observations about political power until such time as we could unanimously agree on what power was, we would never make any observations at all. Even if agreement could be reached, it is undesirable to be wedded to a particular definition before one begins observing events in the real world. Rigid and inflexible definitions of what we expect to find can impede our ability to perceive what really exists. If we think we know what power is, even before we begin our investigations, we are likely to have such impenetrable blinders that we may never understand the phenomenon under study.

Arguing about definitions can also have an invidious consequence. Definitions are all too frequently used to constrain inquisitive hypothesizing and to conceal points of controversy that should be propositionally stated and subject to test.[5]

Ultimately, definitional debates do nothing to improve our familiarity with the empirical world or our understanding of how that world operates. Consider, for instance, the philosophical debates on the status of Buddhism, which has no God and invokes no supernatural deity. Is Buddhism to be considered a religion or should it be considered a philosophy?[6] Any resolution to the question would be strictly arbitrary. It would tell us only about our own definitions and categorical schemes, but little or nothing about the phenomenon ostensibly under study. Definitional debates are usually arguments about labels. They rarely help us understand the operational dynamics of the phenomenon being categorized.

In this sense Pareto was the quintessential empiricist. He urged readers not to start with assumptions about what "must be" or "ought to be." Concentrate instead on observable facts. Simply look for what is.[7] The same can be said for scientific method and epistemology. A science will never progress if all the issues must be resolved before investigation begins.

Advancing Hypotheses Without Inhibition

If the first stage in the scientific process is to make empirical generalizations, the second stage is to advance tentative hypotheses. For Pareto, a hypothesis is a statement of covariance noting that a change in one variable is systematically related in some way to change in one or more other variables. Familiar cases from the physical sciences are $F=M*A$ and $E=mc^2$. That is, we note that when one thing happens, a set of consequences can often be predicted. Let us consider some examples that we can introduce now and discuss in more detail in the passages that follow.

(1) When water is heated, its volume tends to expand.
(2) When people do not receive the rewards they expected, they tend to get angry.
(3) When two groups conflict, the level of cohesion within each group then tends to increase.

People are always afraid to commit themselves to something that may be rejected. But science cannot move forward unless people allow themselves to advance tentative hypotheses and select the ones that best fit observable reality as captured by our empirical observations.[8] This selection among available hypotheses is the third stage in the scientific enterprise.

Selecting Among Alternative Hypotheses

Care is to be exercised when one is choosing to retain (at least tentatively) some hypotheses and reject others. It is not necessary that statements of covariance always be true. Few are strictly true because the universe is a complex system of interdependent parts where multiple causality prevails. The examples introduced in the previous section should exemplify this point. Water heated to 88^0F at sea level occupies less volume (not more) than water heated to 86^0F at 10,000 feet. This is because temperature is not the only thing that influences volume; pressure also influences volume. Many other factors do as well, including the number and types of impurities in the water. Water is rarely pure H_2O. Normal drinking water contains significant quantities of sodium and other dissolved substances that alter boiling point. Sea water contains impurities in far greater concentration. Given that multiple causality prevails, truly accurate predictions can rarely be made on the basis of a single independent variable like temperature.

Consider as well, the social science examples already introduced. It is true that people generally become angry when they fail to receive rewards they had expected. But a person who sustains minor losses during a time of disaster may be overjoyed that his or her losses were limited and contained. That individual might even be extremely thankful in light of the misfortune of others. A family made homeless by a tidal wave is indeed blessed (and may feel so) in comparison with families who have lost lives. And consider our third example: Although groups or collectivities often experience increased solidarity as a result of friction with rivals, units engaged in external conflict can also be torn asunder by the domestic privations that conflict brings. It is more than coincidence that the Russian Revolution of 1917 emerged during the ravages of World War I.

The facts that water heated to 88° F may occupy less volume than water heated to 86° F, that one person experiencing a shortfall between expected and actual outcomes may be happier than a person who does not experience a gap, and that some groups engaged in conflict become less rather than more cohesive, do not constitute a clear invalidation of the original hypotheses. Good scientific experiments always have controls. The whole purpose of a laboratory is to limit the intrusion of external stimuli because scientists are fully aware that multiple causality prevails in the real world. Thus, every hypothesis positing that changes in a and b are associated with changes in c is advanced with the proviso "other things being equal." A single principle, even if it is valid, cannot be expected to yield accurate predictions of events under all circumstances and conditions, because of multiple causality and the endless array of events that can influence outcomes. Nor does the articulation of a succinct principle suggest that scientists have simplistic minds. The concept of experimental control is an essential ingredient in scientific development.[9]

Pareto is quite emphatic on this point. The argument that the social sciences have no general principles is nonsense and reveals a real lack of sophistication on the part of those who raise the issue. People who know anything at all about science recognize that theoretical principles only yield accurate predictions in settings that are, like laboratories, essentially devoid of extraneous stimuli. The fact that there are exceptions to every law when extraneous factors are not controlled does no more to invalidate social scientific principles than it does to invalidate principles in the natural sciences.

> Such nonsense acquires and holds prestige because it chances to accord with the sentiments and the ignorance of the people who listen to it. That explains why "historians" in the field of economics are able with little or no opposition to continue repeating, like parrots, that economic and social laws suffer "exceptions," whereas, they say, scientific laws do not. They do not know, they do not even suspect that their "exceptions" are nothing but phenomena due to the operation of causes alien to those which science, by its process of abstraction, chooses to consider, and that such interposition of alien causes is as commonplace in chemistry, physics, geology, and all other sciences, as it is in economics and sociology. The differences are quite other than they imagine. They lie in the degree of difficulty experienced in separating in the abstract, or even materially, certain phenomena from certain other phenomena. Among such differences in degree it is interesting to note that sciences such as geology, which have to rely chiefly on observation (as distinguished from experiment), cannot separate one phenomenon from other phenomena materially, as do sciences such as chemistry, which are in a position to make extensive use of experiment (as distinguished from simple observation). From that point of view, political economy and sociology are more like geology than like chemistry.[10]

When the French chemist Jacques Charles discovered in 1802 that temperature and pressure are related (Charles's Law is that the volume of a gas is proportional to temperature when pressure is constant), it in no way invalidated Robert Boyle's discovery of 1661 (Boyle's Law is that the volume of a gas is inversely proportional to its pressure). Charles's Law was merely an improvement upon Boyle's law; a closer approximation to empirical reality. Multiple causality is an inescapable feature of the real world. The fact that the world is complex does not lessen the primary obligation of a scientist, which is to reveal by successive approximations the underlying dynamics of the universe.

MODIFYING THE HYPOTHESES WE CHOOSE TO RETAIN

All this is not to say that we should ignore the results when our hypotheses seem to be invalid. Quite the opposite is true. When a hypothesis fails to apply, one tries to ascertain the reasons. This enables us to amend and improve upon theoretical principles, which is the fourth stage of scientific investigation.[11]

One proceeds by conducting experiments to test the applicability of hypotheses in new settings. But in a philosophically pure sense, we do not want verification. A real scientist always searches for cases where our hypotheses seem not to apply. It is in attempting to account for these cases that science expands and improves.

It may be taken by assumption that every scientific hypothesis, proposition, principle, or law can be improved on in some way. This means that disconfirming evidence is always available somewhere.[12] The key is to find disconfirming evidence and recognize the clues that enable us to improve our theories. Each new bit of disconfirming evidence provides another opportunity to modify or supplement our existing hypotheses so that they better capture the operating dynamics of the universe. Or we can reject our previous hypotheses altogether and replace them with something better.[13] In each case we make advances by successive approximation. Our ideas can be tested once they are clearly stated in propositional form, and once they are tested they can be improved upon. Every other science has advanced by successive approximations, in a halting way with starts and stops. There is no reason to assume that sociology will be any different. We must be willing to do the same.[14] Our principles should not be sacred cows shielded from criticism. We should make them explicit precisely so that they can be challenged, improved upon, and ultimately replaced by something better.

THE SYSTEMIC CHARACTER OF REALITY

The social universe can be conceived of as a system.

But however many, however few, the elements that we choose to consider, we assume at any rate that they constitute a system, which we may call the "social system"; and the nature and properties of that system we propose to investigate. The system changes both in form and in character in course of time. When, therefore, we speak of "the social system" we mean that system taken both at a specified moment and in the successive transformations which it undergoes within a specified period of time.[15]

Social systems undergo constant change.[16] And equilibrating forces are at work, so that the society tends to move back toward its characteristic state after abnormal conditions have been introduced.[17]

As we continue improving upon our hypotheses by successive approximations, we hope to understand why systematic patterns emerge. Real success is attained with the development of principles explaining the dynamics of change intrinsic to the kind of system being studied. For instance, Pareto was interested in sociology because he was convinced that economic functions are influenced by certain pervasive sociopolitical dynamics. But he did not call for the replacement of economics because it provides inadequate explanations. He argued instead that other theories, sociological and political theories, should be added to the study of economics.[18] Our understanding of the social universe would thereby improve by successive approximations.[19]

THE LEAP FROM INDUCTIVE TO DEDUCTIVE THEORY

Once the systemic character of the world comes into focus we can begin to identify patterns of action and reaction that follow one another in an unending cycle.[20] If the system analogy holds true, our theories about society should be based on a model of reciprocal determination (change in x produces a modification in y, and change in y produces a modification in x) rather than assertions about unidirectional causality (change in x leads to change in y, but change in y does not lead to change in x). For Pareto's argument is that change in any component of a system has the potential of reverberating throughout the entire system.[21]

Once we have made some progress in this direction, sociologists will be able to marshal the principles they generate through observation and induction into an informative body of deductive theory.

> Social facts are the elements of our study. Our first effort will be to classify them for the purpose of attaining the one and only objective we have in view: the discovery, namely, of uniformities (laws) in the relations between them. When we have so classified kindred facts, a certain number

of uniformities will come to the surface by induction; and after going a good distance along that primarily inductive path, we shall turn to another where more ample room will be found for deduction. So we shall verify the uniformities to which induction has carried us, give them a less empirical, more theoretical form, and see just what their implications are, just what picture they give of society.[22]

In this view, theoretical development is the primary goal of scientific enterprise. The objective of science is to produce a short list of principles that can be used to account for the endless variation one observes in natural environments.[23]

METHODS

Pareto uses observation as his first method. Although some people would take issue with the point, he argues that experience and careful observation of people in their natural settings provide a basis for testing and social scientific experiment.[24] Hence, Pareto used the contemporary social world as one of his laboratories, and he sought to explain his insights with general principles that every person should be able to relate to and consider in application to their own lives. However, Pareto was not the best of writers. His books and essays are often obtuse, so that readers must move through his work carefully and thoughtfully in order to recognize the principles underlying his analysis, and in order to appreciate the contemporary revelance of those principles.

Data

Beliefs and opinions are among the "facts" we can use as evidence. Pareto called these "derivations," or the accounts people make up to represent their feelings and justify their behavior. But "derivations" are not to be taken as true in themselves. People rarely even know, let alone are able to articulate adequately, how they truly feel and why they really do the things they do. Nor can human beings be counted on to actually say what they consciously believe. And in any case, peoples' conscious admissions to themselves may not be reflective of their true subconscious calculations or mental disposition. Derivations are merely useful as indicators, very rough indicators, of each person's underlying "sentiments" or deep-seated values and orientation toward the world.

Observable behaviors, which Pareto called "residues," can also indicate the basic sentiments of a person or group. Yet, real caution

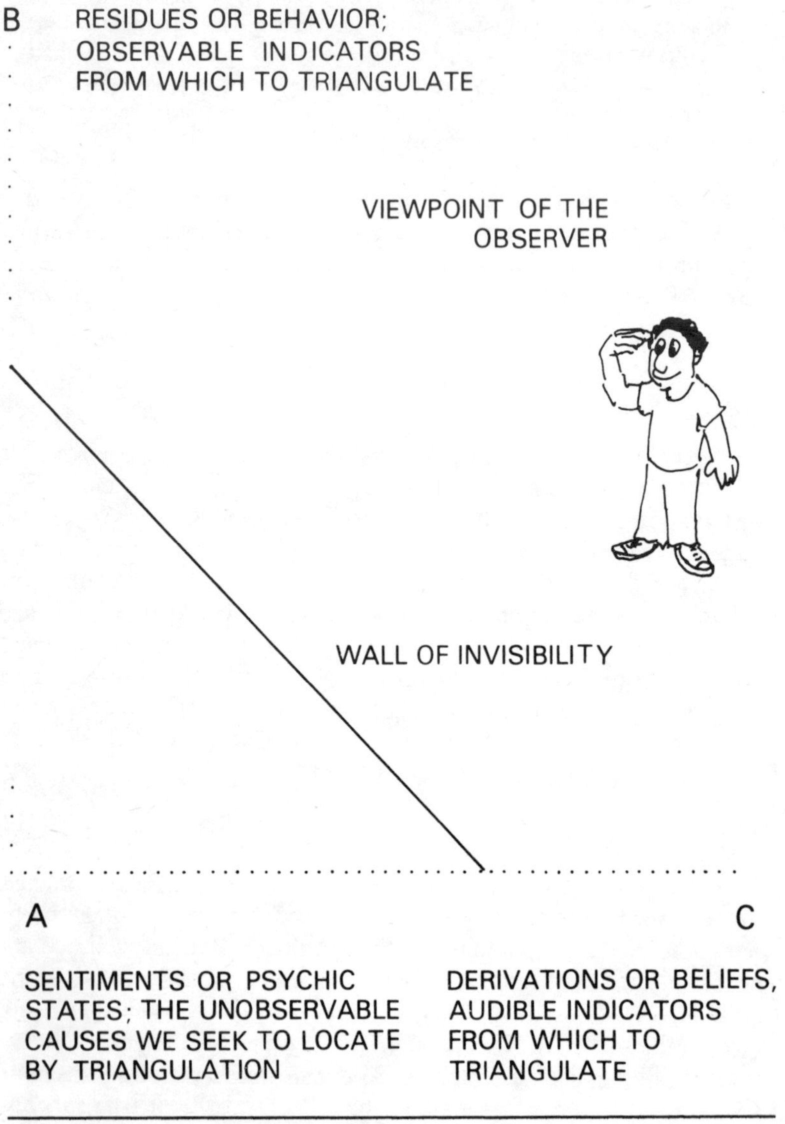

B RESIDUES OR BEHAVIOR;
OBSERVABLE INDICATORS
FROM WHICH TO TRIANGULATE

VIEWPOINT OF THE
OBSERVER

WALL OF INVISIBILITY

A   C

SENTIMENTS OR PSYCHIC   DERIVATIONS OR BELIEFS,
STATES; THE UNOBSERVABLE   AUDIBLE INDICATORS
CAUSES WE SEEK TO LOCATE   FROM WHICH TO
BY TRIANGULATION   TRIANGULATE

Figure 3.1 Pareto's Method of Triangulation

must be exercised. A single behavior might reflect any one of a number of different sentiments or psychic conditions, and a given sentiment or psychic condition might find expression in any one of a number of different behavioral manifestations. It is important to triangulate from different indicators when measuring sentiment.

This means that a good social theorist must be an empiricist. We use the behavior and rituals we observe and the explanations and accounts people relate to us as indicators of the subconscious motivating predilections that are really important.[25] To extend the scope of our data we can look to history for people's past behaviors and to literature and philosophy for literary embodiment of social values and for prevailing explanations of human events. All these data help us gauge the nature of public sentiment characteristic of any particular time and place.

Great caution should always be taken against blind acceptance of the things people say. Rationalized accounts are generated after the fact in order to justify behavior. We cannot treat such ex post facto rationalizations as the causal determinants of their behavioral antecedents. That is, people (individually or collectively) only account for a pattern of behavior after they have started to act in that way. Nor can we assume that behavior will correspond neatly with rationalized story line because any behavior pattern can be justified in many different ways, and many different behaviors can be made to seem reasonable within the same story construction. But we can use behavior and verbal accounts as gross indicators of underlying sentiments that are not directly observable.[26]

All this talk about "residues" and "derivations" is apt to confuse readers. Pareto admittedly used awkward terminology. He was therefore quite insistent that readers avoid the mistake of interpreting terms like "residue" and "derivation" by their common usage in everyday vocabulary.[27] Residues simply refer to the behavior people manifest, and derivations refer to the attitudes, opinions, and beliefs people verbalize. Readers must keep these definitions in mind in order to avoid confusion.

Sociological investigation tends to be limited to observation rather than experiment because we are unable (and thankfully, unwilling) to implement proper experimental controls by denying nonexperimental stimuli to human subjects.[28] But we are able to broaden our concept of observation to include the use of historical records. This has a special advantage, as it is often hard to recognize the truth about matters that are too close at hand. Our prejudices and preconceptions about contemporary matters and the biases we have toward our own customs, culture, religion, and state, make it impossible to be objective observers. It is for this reason that Pareto returns again and again to examples from Greek, Roman, and feudal European history. He uses examples from the distant past because they are least likely to invoke the readers' sentiments, and therefore most conducive to honest reflection and thoughtful analysis of underlying societal dynamics.[29]

Whether based on direct observation or analysis of historical records, our empirical investigations should focus on aggregate data and average patterns. Consider smoking. We know that some cigar enthusiasts smoke more than others. And we know that every smoker indulges his or her habit more on some days than others. Even aggregate national consumption is bound to change with the weather, holiday seasons, and the like. But individual and day-to-day idiosyncrasies are of little importance relative to questions about overall societal patterns. The average aggregate consumption is a social fact of much greater interest to Pareto than the daily habits peculiar to Joe Smith or John Doe.[30]

CAVEATS

Those engaged in the pursuit of knowledge must remember that our body of scientific principles will always be an imperfect guide to understanding. But the current inadequacies of the social sciences are reasons for accelerating our efforts to understand society, rather than reasons to give up in frustration. Nor should the accusations of some, that sociology is nothing but a compilation of common sense, turn us from our course. Critics will decry our efforts while falsely asserting that we have learned nothing. Meanwhile, they take for granted the accumulation of all previous discoveries. They deny social scientists justly deserved credit for these discoveries by claiming that past insights were within the realm of common sense and therefore nothing special, nothing that people did not already know. Alas, the great misfortune of sociology is that the truth about the social world seems painfully obvious once it is pointed out, making it easy for people to assume that they knew such things all along. But that is patently absurd. We are much more knowledgeable about society now than we ever were in the past.

Another pitfall to which sociologists all too often fall victim is the premature desire for application and prediction.

Had Aristotle held to the course he in part so admirably followed, we would have had a scientific sociology in his early day. Why did he not do so? There may have been many reasons; but chief among them, probably, was that eagerness for premature practical applications which is ever obstructing the progress of science, along with a mania for preaching to people as to what they ought to do—an exceedingly bootless occupation—instead of finding out what they actually do.[31]

NOTES

1. Vilfredo Pareto, *The Mind and Society* (hereafter, *Treatise*), Section 20, ed. Arthur Livingston (A. Bongiorno and A. Livingston with J. H. Rogers, trans.) (New York: Harcourt Brace Jovanovich, 1935); reprinted by Dover in 1963 and AMS in 1983 under the original 1916 title, *Treatise on General Sociology*.

2. Ibid.

3. Vilfredo Pareto, *Manual of Political Economy*, eds. Ann Schwier and Alfred Page (A. Schwier, trans.) (New York: August M. Kelley, 1971); translation based on the second edition, originally published in 1909.

4. Pareto, *Treatise*, section 2.

5. Ibid., section 383.

6. Ibid., section 394.

7. Ibid., section 28. For a contemporary exponent of this position, see Robert Dubin, *Theory Building*, 2nd ed. (New York: Free Press, 1978).

8. Pareto, *Treatise*, section 4.

9. Ibid., sections 33, 527.

10. Ibid., section 1792.

11. Ibid., section 34.

12. Ibid., section 69.

13. Ibid., sections 52-55.

14. Ibid., section 2107.

15. Ibid., section 2066.

16. Ibid., section 2067.

17. Ibid., section 2068.

18. Ibid., section 39.

19. Ibid., section 106.

20. Ibid., section 2207.

21. Ibid., section 2060.

22. Ibid., section 144.

23. Ibid., section 826.

24. Ibid., section 6.

25. Ibid., section 162.

26. Ibid., section 169.

27. In much of his work, Pareto refers to sentiments as residues in a kind of shorthand. This is another source of confusion for all but the most careful readers.

28. Pareto, *Treatise*, section 100.

29. Ibid., section 85.

30. Ibid., section 2074.

31. Ibid., section 277.

4

Deflating Logical Explanations
of Conduct

Pareto began his great tome, *Treatise on General Sociology*, just as he had begun his *Manual of Political Economy*, with an epistemological discussion about the requirements of science and techniques for scientific study of the social universe. He then laid out his sociological analysis in a rigorous and systematic fashion. The first element in this argument is that human behavior is nonlogical. It is absolutely essential, in Pareto's estimation, that students of society completely and self-consciously abandon any thought of treating social action as logical, for the assumption of rationality only leads people to erroneous conclusions. This may seem to be a simple and obvious point. But the subliminal tendency to revert to rational explanation is very strong. It frequently creeps into sociological thinking, where it festers and spreads like an unwanted cancer. For this reason, Pareto felt the need to harp on the point, making readers aware of the danger and purging students of any desire to look for logical answers to questions about societal dynamics.

THE PREDOMINANCE OF NONLOGICAL ACTION

Some human behavior is ruled at least in part by logic. For instance, people frequently make cost/benefit calculations in deciding upon a course of action. Economics is, to date, the most advanced of the social sciences precisely because it deals with the domain of semilogical conduct, which tends to be the most elementary and most easily understood kind of action. But most activities are actually nonlogical, and understanding nonlogical action is the main obstacle currently in the way of further social scientific advancement.[1]

Some human behavior is self-consciously nonlogical. For example, many people consider certain numbers to be lucky and powerful, and they regard other numbers as omens of misfortune.[2] Most people admit that these ideas have no rational or scientific claim to validity. And yet, more than a few of us allow such superstitions to influence our behavior. It is not logical but we sometimes follow our intuition despite logic. Consider, for example, the fact that some tall buildings have no thirteenth floor. This is especially true of those buildings constructed in the early days of the sky scraper era around the dawn of the twentieth century. The numbering system in many old buildings jumps from twelve to fourteen in order to avoid arousing fears in the more superstitious and less courageous among us.

Although each of us admits to some nonlogical behavior, most activities seem logical from the standpoint of the person engaged in the action. "In the eyes of the Greek mariners sacrifices to Poseidon and rowing with oars were equally logical means of navigation."[3] It is hard for the people intimately involved with rituals or habitual behavior to appreciate the nonlogical character of their own actions.

Most of the things that people do seem logical from the viewpoint of the actor. However, only a small percentage of all human action really appears logical from the standpoint of outside observers. Pareto reserves the term "logical" for those actions that seem, from the vantage point of uninvolved people with extensive knowledge on the subject, to link means and ends in a reasonable way. All other behavior is "nonlogical," although not necessarily irrational. There was nothing irrational, for instance, about sacrificing to Poseidon. In fact, caulking a ship and sacrificing to Poseidon seem almost equally reasonable.[4] Taking care to appease Poseidon was only prudent caution. It could do no harm and may have helped by reminding mariners of the dangers involved in travel, by increasing solidarity among the crew, and by giving members some cause for optimism about the ultimate outcome of their voyage. Such rituals can also provide a socially acceptable opportunity to change one's plans. It can be read as an omen if clouds become more threatening during or after the ritual preparation for a voyage. Paying proper heed to an ominous message received from

Poseidon is far more manly and palatable than cowardly canceling a voyage because of personal fear or misgiving in the face of worsening weather conditions.

This brings us to an important conclusion. Because most behavior is "nonlogical," it is generally inaccurate to think of people as following rational calculations based on well-defined or clearly articulated premises. Instead, people are motivated by ambiguous sentiments, inclinations, and psychological drives that operate on a subconscious or semiconscious level. We act in response to these sentiments, but always try to fabricate reasonable explanations for our behavior. "Human beings have a very conspicuous tendency to paint a varnish of logic over their conduct."[5] Thus, we often delude ourselves and others into believing that nonlogical behavior is perfectly reasonable, sensible, and justified.

We have all kinds of theories that hide sentiments, caprice, and happenstance. Criminal sentencing provides a perfect example. "In a word, it may be said that court decisions depend largely upon the interests and sentiments operative in a society at a given moment; and also upon individual whims and chance events; and but slightly, and sometimes not at all, upon codes of written law."[6] Most people insist that the application of the law is equitable. This is why people in the Western world allude to lady justice, blindfolded with the telling scales of a gravitational balance in outstretched hand. But in reality there are great disparities in the number of chances people are given, the quality of evidence required for conviction, the severity of sentences passed, and in the delicacy with which people are treated once they have been processed into the criminal justice system.

PROJECTING RATIONALITY

Taboos, habits, and customs are nonlogical in character. We know this because they are enforced with a kind of moral dread rather than logical justification.[7] Comportment rules are the same. They are purely nonlogical. We are told, "do not do that because it is not nice." But this is not a logical explanation. It is an edict, even though it may also be quite reasonable and desirable.

If taboos and customs originated in some universally recognizable logic, they would be similar the world over. But the opposite is the case. Consider a dripping nose. In England it is highly impolite to sniffle with a runny nose. People are expected to clear their nasal cavity by passing a sharp burst of air from the lungs, using a handkerchief or a kleenex as a waste receptacle for any fluids emitted. But taboos are different in Turkey. There, it is considered highly offensive to use this noisy and vile technique in the presence of other people. To blow one's nose in public is the epitome of incivility. It is a barbarous act.

There is a very real tendency to develop elaborate schemes emphasizing the "logical" character of habits and customs. Socrates made a logical science of virtue. Plato (who was a devoted student of Socrates) and Aristotle (who was a devoted student of Plato, and in later years a teacher of Alexander the Great) were willing to move closer to the truth by acknowledging that each person has certain natural (nonlogical) predilections. But they continued to believe that all action flows as a logical consequence once these character traits are taken as given.[8] St. Thomas moved even closer to the truth, recognizing that it is nonlogical from the standpoint of the individual to be virtuous. But he regarded virtuous action as emanating from a part of the soul having divine inspiration. Hence, virtue comes indirectly from God and is logical in God's ultimate view even if mere mortals are spiritually too frail to perceive that more perfect logic.[9] Notice that a clear pattern thus emerges. Even wise philosophers have a tendency to rationalize actions that are, in truth, nonlogical.

But rationalizing nonlogical action is not the sole preserve of mighty philosophers. Everyone strives to hide their prejudices within a veil of logic. For example, nineteenth-century Western Europeans felt superior to their cousins in other parts of the world and invented Social Darwinism to rationalize views about their own superiority. They found it convenient to assume that societies could be located in relationship to one another on a single linear evolutionary line. Once they made this assumption, it was easy for Social Darwinists to conclude "logically" that commercially developed societies must be evolutionarily superior to other societies, as it made little intuitive sense to argue that the industrializing countries had not evolved as far as those with primitive technologies and undeveloped economies. The problem, of course, rests in building an argument upon an initial assumption that is unfounded. If the assumption (in this case unilinear evolution) goes unquestioned, Europeans can go on from there to develop a "logical" defense for their own prejudices.[10] Let there be no mistake. Such theories only take root because they appeal to sentiments and prejudices, not because of any kind of scientific validity. We concoct what seem like logical explanations because we want to tell ourselves that we are reasonable people. We prefer not to recognize our prejudices for what they are.

Members of the human species seem to have an unquenchable need to concoct "logical" explanations accounting for the way things are. These explanations should be given little credence, because people employ logic in a very lax way and are therefore capable of constructing all kinds of explanations for the same phenomenon. So how much credibility can beliefs have?

Just as a single sentiment can give rise to many different patterns of behavior, a single pattern of behavior can be explained in a variety of different ways, all of which seem reasonable to some audience.[11] Consider explanations for the power of sorcerers. Some argued that witches were disciples of the devil.[12] This seemed a logical premise to many and seemed to legitimate the burning of people at the stake. Other theologians argued, also with apparent logic, that to be possessed was to be used as an unwitting pawn of the devil.[13] In this case it would serve the greater glory of God if these innocent wretches could be saved from the stake and their souls cleansed. All such debates were further complicated by various accounts of divine will. There were those who argued that the Devil had no power except that which God, being all-powerful, permitted it and tolerated for reasons beyond any understanding of mere mortals. And there were accused witches who maintained that they were powerless to harm those who wore the cross and were otherwise worthy of the benevolence of the lord.[14] This argument has interesting implications indeed, for it focuses blame on the victims of sorcery.

Consider the logical explanations advanced to explain why the temple of Vesta in Rome, where the symbolic fire of the hearth was maintained, had to be entrusted to female virgins (the legendary vestal virgins). Dionysius asserted that virgins, never having been "corrupted," were the logical people to tend and protect fire, which was regarded as "pure." Plutarch might be taken to suggest the opposite. He argued that fire is barren and should be symbolically entrusted to those whose wombs will remain barren. Other accounts were also advanced by the Romans. Ovid argued that the Goddess Vesta was a virgin and would insist on being attended to by priestesses like herself. Whereas Cicero, in his own practical way, asserted that those practicing celibacy have foregone typical family obligations and commitments and should therefore be more reliable fire keepers.[15]

Whatever the reason, we know that there was a serious expectation of virginity. A number of priestesses were buried alive after having been accused of bringing crop failure and general woe upon the community by violating their vows.[16] But we still cannot be certain why the temple attendants had to be virgins. Nor can we be certain why they had to be female. Why not male virgins? The resort to logic in order resolve such questions is worse than inconclusive. It is misleading and should always be avoided.

Given that a single pattern of behavior can be accounted for in many different ways, and all with some apparent rationality, we must be cautious about accepting verbal constructions as adequate explanation. Instead, verbal constructions are products and are therefore merely indicators of underlying sentiments.

We need to consider the logical experimental validity of the theories people advance.[17] For instance, is the Gospel according to Saint John to be treated as historical narrative or as allegory?[18] In all likelihood it is both. It may well be that the author himself failed to maintain a clear distinction between the two, for in some cultures facts are relayed allegorically and the media and message become inexorably intertwined.[19] In point of fact, there is no scientific way of answering this question.

> Everybody is firmly convinced that *his* religion (morality, law) is the *true* type. But he has no means of imparting his conviction to anyone else. He cannot appeal to experience in general nor to that special kind of experience represented by logical argument. In a dispute between two chemists there is a judge: experience. In a dispute between a Moslem and a Christian, who is the judge? Nobody.[20]

Nor can you resolve moral issues by reverting from the sacred to the secular. Truth, freedom, peace, equality, contentment, and so on, are metaphysical values. There is no a priori way of establishing the primacy of one over another.[21] Moreover, there is a further complication. All things are relative. "The happiness of the 'destroyer of cities' is certainly not the happiness of the citizens he slays. The happiness of the thief is not the happiness of his victim."[22]

"Natural law" and all the other metaphysical invocations are without logical base when closely scrutinized.[23] And even if something can be logically established with a reasonable argument, it is not necessarily true. Saint Augustine and other learned individuals developed convincing arguments that the world was in all probability flat rather than spherical, and if spherical that life as we know it would be impossible in the Western Hemisphere. After all, how could people possibly live standing on their hands and gathering food with their feet?[24] All this goes to prove a point. Scientists must learn to be astute observers rather than place too much trust in reason.

> Long protracted in science was the reign of the notion that celestial bodies, being perfect, had to move in circles. It finally came to be recognized that that idea was false, or better, nonsensical; and the discovery was made by a method altogether different from Aristotle's— by the empirical observations of Kepler.[25]

If we wed ourselves to a conceptualization of the world that seems logical and reasonable, we will surely be led astray, because reality is neither logical nor reasonable. This is particularly true of social reality and the realm of human behavior.

All this is not to say that religious dogma, political doctrine, and metaphysical thought are bad. Quite to the contrary, "the experimental 'truth' of certain theories is one thing and their social 'utility' quite another, and that the two things are not only not one and the same but may, and often do, stand in flat contradiction."[26] Doctrines have great utilitarian value not because of their empirical validity but because they motivate people to do things that can be beneficial for the society at large.[27]

EMPIRICAL MANIFESTATIONS OF THE SAME SENTIMENT

One sentiment can give rise to all different kinds of behavior. Consider the notion that nature can be controlled by appealing to a supernatural deity.[28] Different rituals and beliefs are found scattered about in different places and are practiced in different time periods. In some areas of Greece, yearly sacrifices were made at an Altar of the Winds. In others, when the dry winds that can devastate a grape crop would commence, two men would tear apart a white rooster, run around vineyards in opposite directions carrying their respective halves, and converge on their point of origin to bury the sacrifice. Virgins on the Isle of Sena used chants to invoke air turbulence.[29] And Virgil sacrificed a black sheep to the Tempest.[30] In return for proper devotions, the Greeks were protected against a Persian invasion by divine winds just as the

Japanese were protected from a Mongol invasion by their own divine wind (the Kamikaze).

The important point to remember is that a single underlying sentiment can give rise to all different kinds of practices. A presumption that proper devotions lead to heavenly intervention spawns a wide variety of religious observances, interpretations, and responses. The Reverend Jim Jones instructed his followers to commit mass murder/suicide when their prayers were not met in Jonestown, Guyana. The Romans, in contrast, might be noted for imbuing their devotions and sacrifices with an element of prudent moderation. "'Accept this wine *which I hold in my hands.'* These last words were added to avoid any possible misunderstanding, and the mistake in particular of offering the divinity by inadvertence all the wine in one's cellar."[31]

Because a single sentiment can produce all different kinds of empirical manifestations, it is a mistake to look for a one-to-one correspondence between different actions, habits, or rituals, and their corresponding sentiments. Actions are very imprecise indicators of underlying beliefs. The meaning of actions is not to be taken at face value. Nor is a change in behavior necessarily associated with a change in sentiment. As we have seen, for example, people motivated by the same desire to please the gods can test new procedures and adopt new rituals over time.

OPINION

People who are convinced they know the truth are loath to entertain other points of view. "Faith is by its very nature exclusive. If one believes oneself possessed of the absolute truth, one cannot admit that there are any other truths in the world."[32] Staunch adherence to beliefs often contradicts all logic, for people are at root sentimental rather than rational creatures.

A variety of factors influence opinion formation. It is always important to consider how events materially affect people, because on some level we all weigh our interests before formulating opinions. But when people explain themselves there is a tendency to hide emotional sentiments and material interests behind a veneer of pseudo-logical reasoning. And we adulterate facts in communication by emphasizing favorable aspects of the people and the things we like and by emphasizing unfavorable aspects of the things and the people we dislike.

People habitually employ vague language designed to sound logical while in reality appealing to the sentiments of others.

Many people have a proclivity for embellishing the truth. Chronicling of events changes as a story passes from one person to another or even as a story is repeated by the same person. "To be altered, a story need not pass from mouth to mouth. It is altered even in a repetition by the same person. A thing once said to be large will become larger in successive accounts, a small thing will become smaller."[33] In fact, embellishment is often a requirement of accuracy in communication.[34]

We are ruled by sentiment in virtually everything that we feel, think, and do. Logical arguments are ex post facto fabrication. Real understanding of the social order must be predicated on awareness of the sentimental nature of our species. One should avoid placing too much credence on the accounts people advance for their own behavior or unfolding events in their own society.

NOTES

1. Vilfredo Pareto, *The Mind and Society.* ed. Arthur Livingston (A. Bongiorno and A. Livingston with J. H. Rogers, trans.) (New York: Harcourt Brace Jovanovich, 1935); reprinted by Dover in 1963 and AMS in 1983 under the original 1916 title, *Treatise on General Sociology.*

2. Ibid., section 182.
3. Ibid., section 150.
4. Ibid., section 319.
5. Ibid., section 154.
6. Ibid., section 466.
7. Ibid., section 322.
8. Ibid., section 280.
9. Ibid., section 282.
10. Ibid., sections 728-731.
11. Ibid., section 217.
12. Ibid., section 203.
13. Ibid., section 206.
14. Ibid., section 203.
15. Ibid., section 747.
16. Ibid., section 755.
17. Ibid., section 368.
18. Ibid., section 369.
19. Ibid., section 775.
20. Ibid., section 376.
21. Ibid., sections 377-378.

22. Ibid., section 441.
23. Ibid., sections 440-444.
24. Ibid., section 485.
25. Ibid., section 501.
26. Ibid., section 843.
27. Ibid., section 445.
28. Ibid., section 218.
29. Ibid., section 189.
30. Ibid., sections 192-193.
31. Ibid., section 223.
32. Ibid., section 6.
33. Ibid., section 646.
34. Ibid., section 645.

5

On Human Nature

What does motivate human behavior, if not rationality? In Pareto's estimation, the most important forces at work in the social universe are sentiments. Sentiments are psychic drives and subliminal inclinations. They are deep-seated values or evaluative standards that often remain subconscious but nonetheless compel people to act. Every person has sentiments that have substantial impact on how one behaves. Being at the core of Pareto's theory, the greater portion of the first half of *Treatise on General Sociology* is an examination of the sentiments that propel our conduct in everyday life.[1]

Societies differ from one another in the extent to which they attempt to foster or extinguish various sentiments, and in the extent to which they encourage or discourage the behavioral expression of those sentiments. It is this fact that lies at the very heart of Pareto's sociology. Societies in which the behavioral expression of one set of sentiments is encouraged, fostered, and promoted, will differ substantially from societies that deny or discourage those same sentiments. On aggregate such differences have an impact on political structure and economic trends. Consequently, analysis of sentiments should figure prominently in our study of societal dynamics.[2]

One important caveat needs to be relayed before continuing. Sentiments are not to be confused with what Pareto called "residues" and "derivations." Residues are observable behaviors. Behavior is only an an indicator of the sentiments people hold. Derivations are the opinions and beliefs people articulate. Like residues, derivations are tell-tale indicators of the underlying sentiments people possess. But residues and derivations are nothing more than raw data. They are only of interest as empirical indicators of sentiments, which are the real objects of our study.

Pareto's original texts are subject to not infrequent misinterpretation by those who fail to read closely, because he often uses the term "residue," as a form of shorthand, when in fact he is talking about sentiments. Pareto does inform the reader that he is doing this.[3] But his treatment nonetheless lends itself to confusion. On occasion, Pareto also interchanges the term "instinct," and on rarer occasion the term "derivation," with sentiment. All four concepts are interrelated. People have certain instinctive drives. These drives can be fostered or discouraged by social convention, leaving people with a set of sentiments that motivate and guide behavior. Our actions (residues) and pronouncements (derivations) can serve as rough indicators of the sentiments we hold. Likewise, aggregate patterns of behavior and systems of popular thought help us determine what the sentiments are that prevail in a particular society and at a given time period.

INSTINCTS

At the very core of Pareto's sociological theories rest certain assumptions about human nature. He begins with the assertion that people have genetically programmed proclivities or instincts. He identifies these as combinations, persistence of aggregates (or group persistences), activity, sociality, integrity, and sex.[4]

Combination is a direct translation of the Italian term *combinazioni*. This means inventive cunning, foresight, and guile. It often connotes deceitfulness as well as creative imagination. Persistence of aggregates connotes a desire to preserve things as they are. It implies stubborn adherence to established ways and vehement defense of habit, tradition, and established order. Activity is the need to be expressive. It includes the desire people have to communicate feelings and to respond to their environments. Sociality is the need for affiliation, membership, belonging, and acceptance. Integrity is the need to promote one's own self-interest, to maintain or improve social status, and to emanate a positive sense of identity. And the final human instinct should require no

TABLE 5.1
Instincts Transformed into Sentiments

Combinations	Inventive cunning, guile, and creative imagination
Persistence of aggregates	Stubborn adherence to established ways and vehement defense of tradition
Activity	The need to act and express feelings
Sociality	The desire for affiliation and acceptance
Integrity	Material self-interest and desire for status and self-identity
Sex	The urge for carnal gratification

explanation. The sex drive expresses itself in the search for carnal gratification.

All six of these urges are regarded by Pareto as instinctive. Of course, each individual differs from every other person, so needs that are overpowering in one man or woman may be quite mild in another. But the very nature of our biological composition means that every person will have some urge for all six kinds of actualization. However, as mentioned earlier, societies differ in the degree to which they encourage or discourage expression of these various sentiments. Moreover, our instinctive needs find different avenues of expression in different cultures and in different historical periods.[5]

Now let us examine the intrinsic basis of human sentiments. Pareto argued that various drives, although stimulated or moderated by social convention and normative definitions of acceptable behavior, are fundamentally instinctive. We should therefore find each drive expressing itself, to a greater or lesser degree, in every society throughout human history.

Class I: Combinations

People have a natural inclination to experiment and combine things. The historian Pliny provided vivid evidence of this proclivity to combine when he reviewed folk remedies for various ailments. Pareto relates a number of these cures.[6] The recommendation for epilepsy was a mixture of hog's organs "dried, triturated, and beaten in sow's milk." The supposed cure for jaundice was "wine in which chicken's feet, previously cleansed in water, have been washed." A presumed remedy for ague relates that "one must wear the longest tooth of a black dog as a charm." Unlike some folk remedies, these do not seem to have any basis in fact. On the contrary, they may actually be harmful. But the one important fact these examples illustrate is that people are always trying things.

When developing a remedy for jaundice, there is no logical reason to select chicken's feet over all the other possible alternatives. If feet are the important ingredients, why not use cat's paws or cow's hooves? If chickens provide the important ingredients, why not use beaks or feathers? Why use animals at all? Why not turnips or seaweed? And why not use milk or whiskey or blood instead of wine for the soaking process? The simple fact is that people feel a certain compulsion to experiment, regardless of logic. This is an innate feature of human character. It is part of our instinctive nature.

We frequently see the same proclivity to experiment at work when discoveries and technological advances are made. New discoveries are often made and new products are often invented either by accident or by people involved in rather mindless efforts to combine. Phosphorus, for instance, was discovered by an alchemist looking for gold. Although phosphorus is a natural element (atomic number 15), it was not known in ancient times. The element was first isolated in 1669 after a chemical reaction occurred when Henning Brandt, a German alchemist, tried to make gold by distilling a mixture of putrid urine and fine white sand.[7]

Superstitions are also good indicators of the human inclination to combine things together in imaginative ways. Many people attach special luck to numbers such as 6 because that was the number of days it took God to create the world. So there are those who believe that 6 must be the "perfect" number. Others prefer 7 because it was on the seventh day that God chose to rest, having completed his cycle of work activity. But who is right? What logical grounds do we have for preferring one number over another? This attachment of luck to numbers is most certainly creative thinking in action and demonstrates just how deep-seated and instinctive the proclivity is.[8]

Class II: Group Persistence or Persistence of Aggregates

Just as people seem to have a natural inclination to combine things into new formulations, there is also a very real tendency to hang on tenaciously to old habits and established traditions.

> After the group has been constituted, an instinct very often comes into play that tends with varying energy to prevent the things so combined from being disjoined, and which, if disintegration cannot be avoided, strives to dissemble it by preserving the outer physiognomy of the aggregate. This instinct may be compared roughly to mechanical inertia: it tends to resist the movement imparted by other instincts. To that fact the tremendous social importance of Class II residues is to be ascribed.[9]

We have social institutions, folklore, customs, conventions and habits, precisely because, on some subliminal level, human beings have a natural propensity to preserve the established order and retain things as they are as nearly as is possible.

It is for this reason that new religions frequently adopt ceremonial elements and practices from earlier religions. Adherence to old faiths dies hard unless the believers are made to feel they are transferring rather than changing beliefs.

> So the Christian Church certainly fought might and main against pagan "superstitions," but with varying success. Some of them were demolished and disappeared. Others could not be conquered, and held their ground. When the Church realized that the resistance was too great, it ended by compromising, and contented itself with giving a new garb—often a very transparent one—to an old superstition.[10]

Examining religious practices was one way Pareto tried to gauge the relative strength of Class I and Class II sentiments in different historical epochs and in different societies. Looking back through history, he noted that Romans retained more deities than the Greeks, and the Greeks gave their gods greater embellishment and were more inclined to anthropomorphize. He regarded this as evidence that the inclination to combine was stronger in ancient Greece and the tendency for things to persist was more noticeable in ancient Rome.[11]

The inclination toward group persistence is perhaps most obvious in nationalism and other forms of more or less blind group affinity. There is a pervasive tendency to presume that anything done by "us," whoever "us" happens to be, is acceptable and justified. But God curses others guilty of the same kinds of atrocities.

> So say the modern peoples who decorate themselves with the title "civilized." They assert that there are peoples—themselves, of course— who were intended by Nature to rule, and other peoples—those whom they wish to exploit—who were no less intended by Nature to obey, and that it is just, proper, and to the advantage of everyone concerned that they do the ruling and the others the obeying. Whence it follows that if an Englishman, a German, a Frenchman, a Belgian, an Italian, fights and dies for his country, he is a hero; but if an African dares defend his homeland against any one of those nations, he is a contemptible rebel and traitor.[12]

What hypocrisy! But it cannot be denied. Blind group feeling is real and even has its value. If nothing else, a sense of attachment to tradition and a desire to preserve the established order make it easier for governments to mobilize resources and develop comprehensive policies.

Class III: Activity

People have a need to act. They may not understand why they have to act. They may not have any confidence that their actions will be effective. But they must act. "In general some more or less fantastic rule determines the choice of combination. The impulse to 'do something' is overwhelming; the fancy sets to work, and finds a way to satisfy it."[13] Action may be wholly unrelated to people's real concerns.[14] For instance, it is fairly common for people to take out their career frustrations on loved ones. And this obviously does no good at all. Of course, there are other examples that are more positive in character. Many people play sports in order to relieve the tension and anxiety that builds up in school or at work. Physical energy is released on opponents or on inanimate objects such as squash balls; this can fill the need people have for aggressive action.

The need to act can express itself in all kinds of interesting forms. Consider religious revivals where people are gripped with passionate fervor. Those attending fundamentalist revivals have been known to fall into a trance and act in all manner of ways, including barking at the moon. Some people can be gripped with such passion that they become completely unaware of events going on around them.[15]

Enforced uniformity may be another reflection of our need to act. On one hand we feel a compulsion to perform exactly as everyone else. If other people behave in a certain manner, wear particular types of clothing, and express a given range of opinions, we generally feel compelled to act in a comparable fashion. Inaction is insufficient. We often feel we must be as much like everyone else as possible in all essential respects.[16]

Nor are we content to let the occasional nonconformist live in peace. Most people feel an irresistible urge to punish deviants and make them conform.

> The human being not only imitates to become like others; he wants others to do likewise. If a person departs from the uniform rule, his conduct seems to jar, and produces, quite apart from any reasoning, a sense of discomfort in the persons associated with him. An effort is made to eliminate the jar, now by persuasion, more often by censure, more often still by force. As usual, there is no lack of logical chatter to explain such procedures; but they originate not in the causes so alleged, but in great

part at least in a sentiment of hostility to violations of uniformity, re-enforced by sentiments of asceticism and other sentiments of that type.[17]

People who fail to conform are generally punished quite severely.

Class IV: Sociality

The human need for sociality has its most simple and commonplace expression in material sharing. "The little girl who dresses up her doll and offers it food is not merely imitating her mother; she is expressing a spontaneous sentiment of her own, as in the case with the swallow that has hatched a brood for the first time and carries food to her nestlings."[18] Sharing reaches its ultimate form in altruistic self-sacrifice.[19] For instance, many soldiers are motivated by a deep-seated sense of commitment when they voluntarily expose themselves to mortal danger, or even certain death, in order to save the lives of comrades. This sociality must be rooted in instinct. It is certainly not rooted in rational calculation of self-interest.

On some level, asceticism may also be a reflection of the need for sociality.[20] Self-denial is usually an austere declaration of membership in a community in which extreme sacrifices had once been called for.[21] The same is true for self-flagellation. Being an ascetic is a declaration of affinity with or membership in a community of believers.

Sharing, altruism, and asceticism are striking expressions of a thirst for belonging. But the same instinctive drive is manifest in all kinds of banal ways every day. In the overwhelming majority of human behavior, people are actively seeking approval from others. "The sentiments of sociality manifested by various sorts of residues are nearly always accompanied by a desire for the approbation of others, or for avoiding their censure."[22]

Class V: Individual Integrity

The most common expression of individual integrity is economic self-interest.[23] Under ordinary circumstances we all want what is materially most advantageous for ourselves. In cases of extreme danger, this takes the form of self-preservation. Of course, the desire for self-protection can assume many different forms. For instance, fear leads some people to want to buy guns, at the same time leading other people to support gun control.[24]

Establishing and maintaining a sense of worth is also an important aspect of individual integrity. We try to make ourselves and others feel as though we are worthwhile. When we are unable to do this by heralding our own accomplishments, we often try to do it by denigrating others.[25] This is not a particularly pleasant or desirable facet of human nature, but it is such an obvious part of our character that it cannot be denied. Stereotypes and scapegoating proliferate when people want to blame others for their problems or seek to make themselves feel superior relative to the person or group being denigrated by the stereotype.[26]

Perhaps what fascinated Pareto most is that the need for personal integrity and feeling superior is often cast in the garb of egalitarian ideology. Speaking of the American Populist Movement at the turn of the century, Pareto noted:

> There are hotels in certain places in the United States where a person cannot have his boots polished because it is an offense against Holy Equality for one person to polish another's boots. But the very people who cherish that lofty doctrine of equality are eager to expel the Chinese and Japanese from the United States; are disgusted at the very thought of a Japanese schoolboy sitting at a desk near a child of theirs; will not allow a Negro to be accommodated at a hotel that they frequent, or ride in a railway coach which has the honour of transporting them. The thing would seem incredible if it were not true—but there are those among these fierce believers in Holy Equality who hold that Jesus died to redeem all men (and they call them "brethren in Christ"), and who give their mite to missionaries to go out and convert people in Africa and Asia, yet who refuse to worship their God in an American church to which a Negro is admitted.[27]

Once again, we see that logic has nothing to do with behavior, as is clearly demonstrated by the fact that people feel no particular need to follow through on the logical implications of the ideologies they profess to believe. In truth, most people have few compunctions at all.

Need for individual integrity also finds expression in remorse for having violated ethical rules or taboos, thus putting oneself outside of the fold by reason of being unworthy. In paying penance we reestablish our sense of belonging and our feeling of self-worth.[28] Ritual purification performs the same function. By washing with water or sand or blood (whatever ritual procedures may call for), we seek to cleanse ourselves of sin.[29] Muslims, for example, must perform ritual ablution by washing in prescribed ways before every prayer (five times a day).

This is why each Mosque is to be built, if at all possible, with a clear spring or fresh water source. If water is unavailable, sand can be used as a ritual substitute. Christian baptism for the removal of original sin is another example of the importance ritual purification plays in the lives of many people.[30] Symbolic purification is a reaffirmation of group membership and an individual confirmation that group doctrine is important and revered.

Ritual absolution and purification have played a prominent role throughout human history. Jason, with the safety of the crew of the Argo in mind, had to halt his voyage long enough to appease the gods with prayer and sacrifice in his effort to be absolved for slaying Absyrtus.[31] And although Catholics do not allow anticipatory purification, Roman merchants asked Mercury for absolution from future sins as well as the sins of the past.[32] In more contemporary terms, people in some parts of the world regard the blood of a martyr (for instance, the blood of Christ for Christians or the blood of Ali for Shiite Muslims) as the ultimate of sacrifices.[33] Among some groups the cleansing process involves pain inflicted in prescribed ways. Self-flagellation is a particularly striking way of confirming group membership and intensifying group commitment.

Class VI: Sex

We have no interest in examining the biological aspects of sex. We are interested in sex only because it is a pervasive drive. As such, it has an impact on human behavior, just as the other drives we have discussed do. Each instinct affects people's actions and each gives rise indirectly to certain modes of thought.[34]

Different attitudes regarding sex gain currency at varying points in time. The Greeks and Romans tended to regard it as simply one more biological need like eating and drinking, although they did tend to be intolerant of adultery by married women.[35] By the time Pareto was writing, norms regarding sex had become rather puritanical. People went to great lengths to prohibit anything the least bit suggestive, and pornographers were punished with severity out of all proportion to the damage they caused in comparison to other sorts of crime. Showing a man and a women alone together and seated on a couch was enough to raise the ire of "decent folk" around the turn of the century.[36] Since that time mores have relaxed a great deal in many parts of the world.

Paradoxically, sex figures prominently in symbolism in most cultures.

Even chastity, as Pareto quotes Renan in noting, "is a form of voluptuousness."[37] In the Semitic religious tradition, including Christianity, great emphasis is placed on celibacy. Virginity is often revered as a sensuous and desirable condition.

Remember that the ultimate concern is not with what people say or do about sex. Our real interest is in the fact that people have deep-seated drives of various kinds, and these drives, rather than logic or reason, are the forces that determine the course of history. Christianity, for example, gained the strength that it did, in part, precisely because of the fact that pagan communities were fragmented over issues of sexual morality.

> Manifestly the idea of St. Augustine and others is that the pagan religion was false because it was obscene. The fact that sex sentiments could be appealed to as arbiters is evidence of their great strength. It is also manifest that the claim so often advanced down to our own time that the world owes its cult of purity to Christianity is untenable. Quite to the contrary, the cult of purity, sincere or hypocritical as it may have been, was a powerful factor in the triumph of Christianity. One need only read the Church Fathers to see at once and unmistakably that in defending their derivations they relied upon sentiments favoring chasity and hostile to sex indulgences, which were quite as current among the pagans as in their own circles. They used those sentiments, indeed, to reach minds which were closed to their theological dogmas, and persuade them that they ought to accept a religion that so well expressed sentiments of which they already approved. Such a thing will not strike the reader as surprising after the many proofs we have given that derivations follow, and do not precede, sentiments, though, of course, they may then serve to reenforce them.[38]

SENTIMENT AS A CAUSAL FACTOR
IN SOCIETAL CHANGE

Once again, it is important to reiterate that each society and every historical epoch varies in the extent to which instinctive human drives are acknowledged, encouraged, and allowed to find expression in forms that are deemed legitimate and acceptable. The climate of social acceptance or disavowal is what Pareto meant by sentiment. In some societies, for instance, the tendency to experiment is cultivated to a high art, and in other societies experimentation is chastised and punished.

Social sentiment regarding something as fundamental as the acceptability of innovation has far-reaching implications for public morality and political economy.

It was Pareto's contention that combinations and persistence of aggregates are the most important sentiments influencing the general form of society. A society that encourages change will differ greatly from a society that reifies tradition. And whatever the balance of sentiments in a given period, a shift in either direction will have many ramifications. There is, moreover, a natural polarity between combinations and persistence of aggregates, so that strength in one tends to be associated with weakness in the other. As one periodically rises, the other characteristically falls.[39]

Class I sentiments, that is the sentiments of combination, can have great social utility. A willingness to combine things in new ways stimulates technological invention, economic entrepreneurship, and diplomatic cunning, as well as general flexibility and ability to adapt successfully to new situations. But if the sentiment of combinations is too strong, inadequate attention will be paid to preserving desirable traditions or obeying the social conventions that mitigate against disastrous activities and act as mortar holding a society together.

Class II sentiments can also be very useful because they discourage impetuous actions that might be a waste of energy or have deleterious consequences. And a certain inclination to adhere to established procedures is necessary if useful novelties and innovations are to be retained and used properly.[40] But if the sentiment of group persistence is too strong, serious deviation will not be tolerated and innovation will be rare.[41]

There are a variety of ways to measure change in combinations and group persistences. But certain ways stand out. The rise of humanitarian philosophies can usually be taken as a sign of the ascendance of combinations and the decline of persistence of aggregates. Conversely, a resurgence of religion generally indicates a decline in sentiments of combination and an ascendance of sentiments of group persistence. Greater freedom in sexual expression also tends to indicate the ascendance of sentiments of combination, and restricted sexual expression signals ascendance of persistence of aggregates. This follows from the fact that certain things tend to come in packages. Inquisitive experimentation, pseudo-logical reasoning, and freedom of sexual expression each receive their greatest encouragement, or at least their most placid toleration, during the same periods. Likewise, Pareto felt that formal religions and primordial "us versus them" feelings of group membership are different things that both tend to flourish at the same time that persistence of aggregates enjoys ascent.[42]

We can look for direct evidence of change in combinations and group persistence by being astute observers of human behavior and careful students of social history. Pareto drew on studies of the classical civilizations for much of his data. "Ancient Greece was a laboratory of social and political experiments and it provides a rich storehouse of observations."[43] Sparta, for instance, was overbalanced with Class II sentiments and could not innovate, whereas Athens was burdened with a disproportionate supply of Class I sentiments and could not capitalize on useful innovations or maintain continuity in programs, policies, or stratagems. Sparta's military practices provide a useful example. Famed though Spartans were for their success on the field of battle, knowledge of Spartan history causes one to raise some questions about the merit of this reputation. Sparta's characteristic strategy was to simultaneously engage each enemy along the entire front on which its army was deployed. Iphicrates of Athens detected the flaw in this battle plan and utterly destroyed a corps of 600 at the battle of Leuctra near Corinth in 390 B.C. It was then that the Spartan command should have reconsidered its military theory, but Spartan attitudes did not sanction deviation from past practices or the innovation of new approaches. Sparta sustained another major defeat when Epaminondas of Thebes concentrated the main body of his army in an attack formation 50 ranks deep (which was a novel innovation) and thrust this formation into a single strategic breach to rout the Spartan force.[44]

This example demonstrates how Pareto approached history through the eyes of a sociologist. Social sentiments were, in his view, major determinants of the course of historical events. But Pareto had to pay closer attention to the problems and pitfalls that one confronts when trying to assess social sentiment. The next chapter relates his treatment of these pitfalls.

NOTES

1. Vilfredo Pareto, *The Mind and Society* (hereafter, *Treatise*), ed. Arthur Livingston (A. Livingston and A. Bongiorno with J. H. Rogers, trans.) (New York: Harcourt Brace Jovanovich, 1935); reprinted by Dover in 1963 and AMS in 1983 under the original 1916 title, *Treatise on General Sociology*, vols. 1 and 2.

2. Vilfredo Pareto, *The Transformation of Democracy*, ed. Charles Powers (R. Girola, trans.) (New Brunswick, NJ: Transaction Books, 1984, chapter 4); originally published in 1921.

3. Pareto, *Treatise*, section 875.

4. Ibid., section 888.

5. Pareto, *Transformation*, chapter 4.

6. Pareto, *Treatise*, section 894.

7. Ibid., section 899.

8. Ibid., section 962-963.

9. Ibid., section 992.

10. Ibid., section 1001.

11. Ibid., section 998.

12. Ibid., section 1050.

13. Ibid., section 1092.

14. Ibid., section 1089.

15. Ibid., section 1098.

16. Ibid., section 1119.

17. Ibid., section 1126.

18. Ibid., section 1150.

19. Ibid., sections 1145-1148.

20. Ibid., section 1171.

21. Ibid., section 1175.

22. Ibid., section 1161.

23. Ibid., section 1207. Also see Vilfredo Pareto, *Manual of Political Economy* (New York: August M. Kelley, 1971); translated from the second edition, originally published 1909.

24. Pareto, *Treatise*, section 1218.

25. Ibid., section 1220.

26. Ibid., sections 1224-1227.

27. Ibid., section 1224.

28. Ibid., section 1241.

29. Ibid., section 1247.

30. Ibid., section 1289.

31. Ibid., section 1254.

32. Ibid., section 1252.

33. Ibid., section 1281.

34. Ibid., section 1324.

35. Ibid., section 1325.

36. Ibid., sections 1326, 1345.

37. Ibid., section 1331, footnote 1.

38. Ibid., section 1341.

39. Pareto, *Transformation of Democracy*.

40. Pareto, *Treatise*, section 2420.

41. Ibid., section 2433.

42. Vilfredo Pareto, *The Rise and Fall of the Elites* (introduced by Hans Zetterberg) (Totowa, NJ: Bedminster Press, 1968); originally published 1901, chapters 2 and 3.

43. Pareto, *Treatise*, section 2419.

44. Ibid., section 2434.

6

Popular Beliefs

Students of society always feel greatly tempted to seek insights and understanding from the opinions that popularly prevail, the ideologies that hold sway, and the dogmas that dominate in a given era. But there is great danger in this, because the explicit content of all of popular beliefs tends to be nothing more than ideological or cosmetic veneer. Although it is true that common people attach great meaning to popular beliefs and repeat their myths with apparent enthusiasm and commitment, a careful study of history reveals that what really motivates people is rarely what they verbally profess. There is, therefore, a great danger in taking anything that people say too literally. If we are to attach any meaning at all to philosophy or ideology, it should be after considering them in a circumspect manner and finding the underlying sentiments they manifest.

DERIVATIONS DEFINED

As we discussed in Chapter 4 on nonlogical action, derivations are the opinions, beliefs, ideologies, philosophies, or story lines people advance in order to portray their behavior as reasonable and in order to gain the support of others by appealing to common sentiments. Derivations obscure true motives, even to the people directly involved.[1] They are "the ways in which people try to dissemble, change, explain, the real character of this or that mode of conduct."[2]

DERIVATIONS AS CAMOUFLAGE
FOR MATERIAL INTERESTS

It is important to realize that people are always inclined to use some appeal to sentiment in order to conceal their true motives and in order to allow them to do what they find rewarding or tantalizing. The six Crusades to the Holy Land (occurring in the years 1096-1099, 1147-1149, 1189-1192, 1202-1214, 1218-1221, and 1228-1229) provide a good example. All six ventures resulted in a costly drain of men and material from the West. All six were justified to the civilian population of the West in the name of lofty ideals. And all six were characterized by a good deal of barbarous pillage and devastation visited in the name of the Prince of Peace.[3] Only the ill-fated "Children's Crusade" (of 1212 A.D.) seems to have been inspired by noble goals to the exclusion of desire for material profit on the part of all the various participants. People acting in the name of religion have no monopoly on weakness in the face of material temptation. Consider the detractors of religion.

> Something very similar was observable during the Reformation, when many German princes were rather more attentive to appropriating Church properties than to interpreting the Scriptures, ever regarding as the soundest text the one that brought the desired goods into their hands with the least trouble.[4]

True piety would seem to be a very rare commodity.[5] The easiest way to justify behavior is by making it seem as though one's actions and interests are allied with values people are unwilling to challenge. Appeals to values like progress and virtue are always popular among greedy charlatans.[6]

In the final analysis it must be realized that derivations are just tools people use to justify their actions. The supposed logic is ignored if it does not suit one's interests. Governments are by far the worst perpetrators of this kind of immorality. "A glance at history is enough to show that natural law is just a rubber band: the powerful can stretch it to whatever length they choose."[7] In 1913 the British insisted that Albania retain its independence from Montenegro, and they used military force to ensure that their will prevailed. The British position was based on an appeal to "Natural Law," arguing that Albanians were ethnically, religiously, and linguistically distinct and should therefore be allowed their independence. But in 1913, the British would never have considered applying the same principle to foreign domination of the Indian subcontinent. The superpowers do what they please and justify it with grand phrases.

Imperial Russia performed the same feat of logical manipulation. They attacked the Turks for failing to assimilate or integrate certain nationalities in occupied territory, but would never have applied the same criteria of success to their own occupation of Poland. The truth is that Turkey was weak at the time and most Europeans were happy with any pretext they could find to legitimate intervention and share in the spoils resulting from dismemberment of the Ottoman Empire. It might be noted that Pareto was one of the few opinion leaders of his time to speak out against Italy's colonial war (in 1911) with Turkey.[8]

All this is not to say that people consciously perpetrate deceit on others. Most people are earnest enough and have good intentions. Unfortunately though, there seems to be a human tendency toward self-deceit.

> The schemer consciously aims at m and preaches: T; but the same thing is also done by many individuals who are in all good faith. Cynically selfish people are rare and downright hypocrites equally so. The majority of men merely desire to reconcile their own advantage with the residues of sociality (Class IV); realize their own happiness while seeming to strive for the happiness of others; cloak their self-seeking under mantles of religion, ethics, patriotism, humanitarianism, party loyalty, and so on; work for material satisfactions while seeming to be working only for ideals.[9]

THE ORIGIN OF DERIVATIONS

Those sentiments that really motivate action would exist even without derivations. But for some reason people like having arguments that rationalize and justify the actions they would be inclined toward in any case.[10] It is human nature (Chapter 5) for us to try to convince ourselves and others that our actions are consistent with right thinking and reasonable patterns of conduct.

People seem to assume implicitly that patterns of behavior develop as a result of the kinds of ideology that are popular. But this assumption is in reality rather ludicrous. Rules are created and ideologies are generated after a practice becomes widespread and not before.[11] We see this phenomenon at work in the law. Legal codes and ethical systems change in acknowledgment of, not prior to, the emergence of a new social order.[12] Philosophers, poets, jurists, theologians, and novelists chronicle rather than create new social undercurrents, and in doing so, they facilitate the further spread of concepts that are already gaining currency. The world did not change appreciably because Voltaire and Rousseau were born. Quite to the contrary, their ideas gained popularity because they embodied the attitudes and sentiments of the times.[13]

> Generally speaking, a derivation is accepted not so much because it convinces anybody as because it expresses clearly ideas that people already have in a confused sort of way—this latter fact is usually the main element in the situation. Once the derivation is accepted it lends strength and aggressiveness to the corresponding sentiments, which now have found a way to express themselves.[14]

Focusing on sentiments rather than derivations enables us to understand a great deal about the course of events.[15]

Derivations originate in our desire to be validated. But little can be said beyond that. We can never be sure how the theories of bygone ages actually originated.[16] Nor is discovering the origins of theories the task of sociology. The goal of the sociologist is to ascertain why some ideas gain currency and others do not.

> When the logician has discovered the error in a reasoning, when he can put his finger on the fallacy in it, his work is done. But that is where the work of the sociologist begins, for he must find out why the false argument is accepted, why the sophistry persuades. Tricks of sophistry that are mere finesses in logic are of little or no interest to him, for they elicit no very wide response among men. But the fallacious, or for that matter the sound, theories that enjoy wide acceptance are of the greatest concern to him. It is the province of logic to tell why a reasoning is false. It is the business of sociology to explain its wide acceptance.[17]

There is a real temptation to assume that dogma sways action. But this tends not to be the case.[18] Dogma certainly affects how people organize their thoughts for verbal presentation, but we must always remember that derivations are appeals to sentiments that people already have.[19] And if some logical conclusion is in disharmony with a person's sentiments or material interests then the analysis will be dismissed out of hand and replaced with another.

The clearest examples of what Pareto meant are arguments using words that evoke great emotion but in the final analysis have vague and ambiguous meaning. "Solidarity" is one such word. It means many things to many people. In fact, it can be used to mean almost anything. But regardless of audience or imputed meaning, the word is always used as an appeal to sentiments. It moves people to action solely because it stirs emotions.[20]

Labels are also used to stir the emotions. "Just," "unjust," "moral," "immoral," "right," and "wrong," are just a few examples of the catchwords that people use to guide opinion by coating pseudo-logical arguments in phraseology that activates people's sentiments and makes it difficult to disagree.[21] Pareto notes that Aristotle's advice is: "If one would favour a thing, the metaphor must be chosen from what is best; if one would harm it, from what is worst."[22] This is why government supporters refer to revolutionaries as terrorists and murders, whereas police are defenders of liberty. For rebel sympathizers in disaffected communities, revolutionaries might be the defenders of liberty and police may be regarded as terrorists and murders. Neither viewpoint can be said to be right or wrong based on any scientific or universal standard of evaluation. These are issues pertaining to emotion and sentiment rather than questions of fact or logic.

When our opponents cloak their arguments in terms evoking positive sentiments, we can envelop our own position in double positives. If our opponents profess to want freedom, we can cry out for *true* freedom.

> To take a drink of wine when you choose is just "freedom"—it was the freedom the Czar granted to the Finns. To be forbidden to touch lips to a drop of wine is "true freedom"—it was the freedom the "liberal" assembly of Finland would have granted to that country had it not been prevented from doing so by the Czar's despotism.[23]

DIRECT CORRESPONDENCE (OR LACK THEREOF) BETWEEN DERIVATIONS AND BEHAVIOR

There is no one-to-one correspondence between any given pattern of behavior and the derivations used to account for it. Any one of a number of derivations could be developed in order to encourage or discourage a given behavior. For example, derivations that could be advanced against murder would include (but would by no means be limited to) a taboo against shedding blood, God's law, ethical prescriptions about treating others as you would have them treat you, formulas for promoting the best interests of the tribe, assumptions about ritual contamination occurring in the presence of dead bodies, the pessimistic assumption that life would be a worse fate for your enemies than death, and fear of the ghost or protective spirits of the potential victim.[24] This is only a small sampling of the kind of pseudo-logical explanations that have been advanced in order to account for prohibitions against murder. The simple fact is that different groups have different explanations for the same norm.

> A Chinese, a Moslem, a Calvinist, a Catholic, a Kantian, a Hegelian, a Materialist, all refrain from stealing; but each gives a different explanation for his conduct. In other words, it is a case of a number of derivations connecting one residue that is operative in all of them with one conclusion which they all accept.[25]

There often seems to be an independence between how people live and what they purport to believe. All kinds of loyal churchgoers and purveyors of piety are brigands and rogues once the sabbath has passed.[26] Human beings are adept at glossing over contradictions between doctrine and behavior.[27] This is probably because people find it so easy to view themselves as being in the right. Our ideologies blame victims when we are advantaged and blame the advantaged when we are downtrodden. Complicity in oppression of all kinds can be made to seem innocent with the proper verbal gymnastics.

REQUIREMENTS (AND LACK THEREOF) FOR PROOF AND LOGICAL CONSISTENCY

Wherever faith prevails, people have little need for proof that their theories are accurate or logically consistent.[28] Aspects of religious doctrines can be implausible or contradictory[29] without shaking people's faith.[30] Indeed, as scientists shatter old conceptions about the universe the faith of many people seems to deepen rather than erode. How vast and wondrous the world is, and how glorious the miracle of human life. The more that scientists reveal about the world, the more glorious God seems to believers.

There is no surprise in the fact that agnostics feel supported in their views by the same body of scientific discovery, and nonbelievers sometimes appeal to science in an effort to challenge the faith of others. But a person who challenges derivations usually only convinces those who were of the same persuasion all along.[31]

Each side in every conflict believes itself to be on the side of God, righteousness, and justice. Homer's gods were invoked by both the Greeks and the Trojans at the moment of their encounter. And the Germans and the French both felt confident that God was on their side in 1870. "So, besought for aid by two opposite sides, 'eternal Justice' did not know which way to turn and ended by preferring the side that had the larger army and the better prepared, and was led by the better generals."[32]

LONGEVITY OF DERIVATIONS

A derivation that lasts for a long time is not necessarily true. But longevity does suggest that the sentiments underlying a given derivation are probably strong. On the other hand, changes in derivations do not necessarily indicate that sentiments are weak. New derivations can be readily adopted should old ones lose acceptance for any reason. For instance, a nation at war may decide that killing is acceptable under the "proper" circumstances; that is, as long as the killing remains exogenous. If murder had once been proscribed on the basis of a taboo against the shedding of human blood, a society at war can be expected to conjure some other derivation (e.g., a taboo against harming one's "brother") to rationalize prevailing behavioral norms without discouraging military combat. Human beings tend to be very practical in their use of derivations. If one derivation proves inconvenient, for whatever reason, another will be invented for the same purpose.

DERIVATIONS AS DATA REVEALING TRUE SENTIMENTS

Derivations are often quite entertaining and their superficial aspects can occupy our attention. "We must not, however, stop at derivations.

We have to go on to look for the sentiments that they veil."[33] We can do this by sharpening our powers of empathic analysis and looking for underlying meaning.

> How could we still enjoy the poems of Homer and the elegies, tragedies, and comedies of the Greeks and Latins if we did not find them expressing sentiments that in great part at least, we share? Aeschylus, Sophocles, Euripides, Aristophanes, Plautus, Terence, Virgil, Horace, and other writers of Graeco-Latin antiquity—are they foreigners whom we no longer understand? Do we not find in Thucydides, Polybius, Tacitus, and other ancient historians, descriptions of things that reveal, under different, sometimes very different, guises, a fund of human sentiments identical with what we observe today?[34]

Similarities in the underlying messages being communicated reflect a basic stability in the instinctive characteristics of our species. At the same time, pendulous variation in the messages being communicated reflects the cyclical changes that occur in social sentiment, as society first tries to encourage and then discourage each of the various drives with which mankind is somehow predisposed. Consider sociality and the corresponding demand for conformity. Many Christian communities used to provide every possible "encouragement" for religious uniformity. In Puritan areas of New England people accused of witchcraft were not infrequently burned at the stake. These same communities now show a far greater degree of religious tolerance. Sentiments have changed. And yet, this is not to say the demand for conformity is now altogether absent. It simply does not receive as much social stress now as it did in the seventeenth century.[35]

The sentiments underlying any given trend or set of actions are rarely obvious. The verbal pronouncements of Luther, Calvin, and other figures in the Reformation might lead one to believe that Protestantism was a liberalizing movement. The theological arguments were based, after all, on an appeal for individual involvement and the acceptance of individual responsibility for scriptural interpretation. But at the time the entire movement was, at least in Pareto's view, a conservative backlash. It represented a groundswell of common dissatisfaction with changing doctrinal interpretations in the Catholic church.[36]

Indeed, derivations are frequently used to hide the real truth about societies. Every country claims to be a democracy, but few societies really are. This is what Pareto meant when he said: "We need not linger or the fiction of 'popular representation'—poppycock grinds no flour."[37] Many regimes hold elections but deny people any real choice of candidates. Other regimes profess to tolerate free thinking but restrict private ownership of typewriters or access to duplicating machines. All governments claim to be benevolent, but tyranny abounds.

By paying careful attention to the underlying meaning of derivations, we are able to locate a trend line showing periodic shifts in sentiment. Pareto concluded that such shifts represent a pendulous cycle.[38] In tracing this cycle, care must be taken to ensure that a sufficient span of time is examined and an adequate number of measurements taken at intervening time points. A thoughtful examination of social sentiment (as revealed in derivations) will demonstrate a great deal about a society and provide some grounds on which to make predictions about the future. This is especially true if we are willing to inform ourselves about patterns of past events. Pareto believed, for example, that studying the decline of Rome would suggest valuable insights that have contemporary relevance.[39]

PRACTICAL USES OF DERIVATIONS

Why do some derivations gain currency? There are a number of reasons owing to our basic human qualities. Our need for sociality encourages us to accept ideas propounded upon by persons in authority,[40] and encourage us to conform to customary practice and belief.[41] Derivations can also be used to confuse individual interests with normative behavior so that the two seem to blend.[42] So derivations can help to define and bolster the traits people in a given society choose to encourage.

Keeping all this in mind, it is reasonable to acknowledge that politicians use derivations to arouse the sentiments of the people. This is not necessarily immoral or unethical. On the contrary, it is a necessary part of the art of politics. Otto von Bismarck, for instance, was a great statesman and successful politician because he understood how to arouse and manipulate popular sentiment.[43] An effective politician does this just as Cicero did, by associating his or her cause with vague adjectives that people are unwilling to reject.[44] "Ruling-class theories, when the requirement of logic is not too keenly felt, appeal simply to sentiments of veneration for holders of power, or for abstractions such as 'the state,' and to sentiments of disapprobation for individuals who try to disturb or subvert existing orders."[45] Derivations stir up sentiments and incite people to act in the ways they are already predisposed to act.[46]

FORCES OF CHANGE

Theories undergo constant change as people try to deal with inconsistencies between doctrine and the nature of the real world.[47] "As regards derivations, they overstep reality, as a rule, in the direction in which they are headed, whereas they rarely stop short of it."[48] There is a definite tendency for sentiments to go to an extreme and for derivations to follow and accelerate the process. We have now arrived at the heart of Pareto's theory: forces giving rise to cyclical oscillation in social sentiment. His theory of sentiment is the subject of the next chapter.

NOTES

1. Vilfredo Pareto, *The Mind and Society* (hereafter, *Treatise*), ed. Arthur Livingston (A. Bongiorno and A. Livingston with J. H. Rogers, trans.) (New York: Harcourt Brace Jovanovich, 1935); reprinted by Dover in 1963 and AMS in 1983 under the original 1916 title, *Treatise on General Sociology*.

2. Ibid., section 1397.
3. Ibid., section 1462.
4. Ibid., section 2517.
5. Ibid., section 2518.
6. Ibid., section 1463.
7. Ibid., section 1689.
8. Ibid., section 1708.
9. Ibid., section 1884.
10. Ibid., section 1401.
11. Ibid., chapter II.
12. Vilfredo Pareto, *The Transformation of Democracy*, ed. Charles H. Powers (R. Girola, trans.) (New Brunswick, NJ: Transaction Book, 1984, pp. 48-49); originally published in 1921.
13. Pareto, *Treatise*, section 1763.
14. Ibid., section 1747.
15. Ibid., section 2520.
16. Ibid., section 1402.
17. Ibid., section 1411.
18. Ibid., section 1543.
19. Ibid., section 1546.
20. Ibid., section 1557.

21. Ibid., section 1551.
22. Ibid., section 1552.
23. Ibid., section 1561.
24. Ibid., section 1414.
25. Ibid., section 1416.
26. Ibid., section 1745.
27. Ibid., section 1817.
28. Ibid., section 49.
29. Ibid., section 1450.
30. Ibid., section 1454.
31. Ibid., sections 1455-1456.
32. Ibid., section 1951.
33. Ibid., section 1716.
34. Ibid., section 1719a.
35. Ibid., section 1715.
36. Ibid., section 1701.
37. Ibid., section 2244.
38. Ibid., section 1718-1719.
39. Ibid., section 1799.
40. Ibid., section 1445.
41. Ibid., sections 1448-1449, 1468.
42. Ibid., sections 1477-1479.
43. Ibid., sections 1843, 1866.
44. Ibid., section 1906.
45. Ibid., section 2182.
46. Ibid., section 2201.
47. Ibid., sections 2007-2008.
48. Ibid., section 1772.

7

Toward a Theory of Social Sentiment

Sentiments, as reflected by residues and derivations, are important determinants of social structure and change.[1] In this chapter we will advance a theory of sentiments to account for the constant oscillation between periods of what might be called liberalism and conservatism that is observable throughout history.[2] The chapters that follow will note how these cyclical changes in sentiment interact with other forces to influence economic trends and patterns of political organization, thus altering the overall form of the society. This analysis suggests the kind of "general sociology" Pareto envisioned. We are moving step by step toward our goal of understanding Pareto's theories regarding social equilibrium and societal change.[3]

PARETO'S TERMINOLOGY AND ASSUMPTIONS

It is important to avoid confusion about Pareto's use of terms. This is especially good advice for those students who move, as indeed everyone should, beyond secondary reviews like this one and read Pareto in the original. The real foci of Pareto's analysis are sentiments, or underlying value orientations and psychic conditions. These are not directly observable. But what people say (derivations) and what people do (residues) can be recorded and used as indirect measures of social sentiment. Sometimes Pareto says "residue" or "derivation" when he really means "sentiment." This is a form of shorthand notation used because, ever the good empiricist, Pareto never wanted to lose sight of his empirical indicators. "Returning to the matter of our modes of expression, we must further note that since sentiments are manifested by residues we shall often, for the sake of brevity, use the word 'residues' as including the sentiments that they manifest. . . . Derivations also manifest sentiments."[4]

It is as if our neighbors have brick walls impeding our ability to look in and discover what they are really thinking. However, we can see a portion of their public behavior and hear some of what they say, and these behaviors and utterances reflect cognitive processes occurring inside the person. Both reflect the operation of unobserved processes behind the brick wall of which we figuratively speak. Once we recognize this, it becomes clear that our real task is to use actions and utterances as data and try to deduce the sentiments and psychic processes from which they originate.[5] This is not an easy task.

> Even a very superficial view of present society reveals streams of opinion that manifest underlying patterns of sentiments and interests. These underlying sentiments and interests [rather than opinions about specific issues] are the forces at work determining the character of social equilibrium. We must therefore avoid becoming overly preoccupied with exactly what people say, at the expense of our interest in the underlying sentiments which those indicators reflect. And because we are interested in aggregate patterns of sentiment, we should avoid preoccupation with highly unusual outlying cases.[6]

That must not be forgotten. Behavior and utterances are merely data; they are not the objects of our study. Sentiments are the objects of our study.

Change in sentiment is one of the principal factors capable of altering the course of events in society. Pareto reached this conclusion while writing commentary on the political economy of Italy, but his observations are confirmed again and again in studies of history. Every society moves through successive periods of ascendancy and decay, faith and skepticism, economic growth and decline, political centralization and fragmentation. Shifts in sentiment are major elements in this inexorable cycle.[7]

Our focus, then, is on patterns of change in popular sentiment or social mood. These social phenomena oscillate as do trends in the economy,[8] and the goal of this chapter is to advance a theory accounting for the observed pattern of oscillation. We do this by noting the forces producing change in attitudes and mores. Our observations will enable us to articulate a set of theoretical principles accounting for changes in sentiment.[9]

FIRST OBSERVATION: SENTIMENTS OSCILLATE

It is clear that societies do differ from one another. Lasting differences are lumped together in most people's minds and colloquially referred to as culture. Pareto argued that the crux of cultural variation is attributable to differences in receptivity to change. "The differences between Sparta, Athens, Rome, England, and France that we have noted in Chapter II were nothing but differences in intensities of Class I and Class II residues."[10] Sentiments fostering combination (innovation) and group persistence (adherence to tradition) are always at work. But every society legitimates and encourages these two inclinations to different degrees. If one sentiment is particularly strong, the character of the society will be affected. If one is particularly weak, making the other strong in relative terms, the character of the society will also be influenced. Hence, any change, an increase in one or a decline in the other, has impact on the direction of future events.

Let us grant that cultures do differ from one another but that we are presently unable (or at least that Pareto was unable) to explain why people in one society tend, over a period of generations, to be more receptive to change than people in another society. However, Pareto's contribution rested in an analysis of change within a given society over time. If we take a single society as our unit of analysis, we know that sentiments change over time and that these changes have a profound impact on the course of socioeconomic and political events.

This brings us to an important point. Pareto's first pivotal observation about history is that every society alternates between periods when change is encouraged (at least relative to the norm for that society) and other periods when adherence to tradition is demanded (again, at least relative to the norm for that society). Hence, popular mood can be said to oscillate. We see the same pattern of change in all nations. The median point may differ from one society to another but no society ever remains stationary at that point. Whatever the average propensity to legitimate or discourage change, there is waffling back and forth as people show first more, then less tolerance than is modal for that culture.[11] "Hence those perpetually recurrent swings of the pendulum, which have been observable for so many many centuries, between skepticism and faith, materialism and idealism, logico-experimental science and metaphysics."[12]

Pareto sought to explain why sentiments oscillate. Furthermore, he was convinced we would eventually be able to predict the timing, direction, duration, and magnitude of social change. History reveals that social sentiments oscillate in a pendulous and unending fashion. Identifying these recurrent swings provides concrete cases for us to ponder and around which to begin to build a theory.

> And so it is, considering for the moment only one or two of such oscillations, that in a little more than a hundred years, and, specifically, from the close of the eighteenth to the beginning of the twentieth century, one witnesses a wave of Voltairean skepticism, and then Rousseau's humanitarianism as a sequel to it; then a religion of Revolution, and then a return to Christianity; then skepticism once more—Positivism; and finally, in our time, the first stages of a new fluctuation in a mystico-nationalist direction. Leaving the natural sciences aside and keeping to social theory, there has been no notable progress in one direction or the other. In a word, if faith is just a harmful prejudice, how comes it that it has survived over so many centuries, constantly reshaping itself and constantly reappearing, after its enemies, from Lucretius on, had thought they had vanquished it for all time? And if scientific skepticism is really so futile, so inconclusive, so harmful to human society, how comes it that it can return to fashion every so often in the plain good sense of a Lucian, a Montaigne, a Bayle, a Voltaire?[13]

A clear pattern of oscillation emerges if we take care to plot Pareto's observations of changes in social sentiment the way an economist would plot changes in the business cycle. And Pareto's specific examples give us an empirical referent for further study and thought.[14]

SECOND OBSERVATION: SENTIMENTS DIFFER WITHIN EVERY POPULATION

Cohort experiences tend to mold popular sentiment and establish parameters for popular response on public issues. This is one reason why Italy was as slow as it was to involve itself in imperial adventure.

Many northern Italians had suffered under the yoke of Austrian domination, and they could sympathize with the viewpoint of colonized peoples. But as a cohort ages, it is replaced by a younger group of people with different experiences, sensitivities, and sensibilities. As 1900 approached, those Italians who remembered the Austrian presence were dying off and being replaced by citizens who had no memory of foreign domination. This made it easier for the Italian government to militarize, invade Arab territory, establish a quasi-colonial sphere of influence in the Adriatic Sea, and engage in various incursions into Ethiopia.[15] We see something comparable now happening in the United States. New Deal social welfare and economic maintenance legislation was ushered in by voters and politicians (e.g., Lyndon Johnson and Hubert Humphrey) who were adults when the Great Depression struck. That generation is sympathetic to the plight of the downtrodden, because it is painfully aware that hard times can arrive through no fault of the individual. But as the depression generation ages, we are seeing a deemphasizing shift in welfare policies and programs.

Another important observation is that social sentiments tend, on aggregate, to differ by economic class. So our concern with sentiments is not always restricted to the analysis of society as a homogeneous agglomeration.

> Residues are not evenly distributed nor are they of equal intensities in the various strata of a given society. The fact is a commonplace and has been familiar in every age. The neophobia and superstition of the lower classes has often been remarked, and it is a well-known fact of history that they were the last to abandon faith in the religion which derived its very name, paganism ('ruralism') from them.[16]

It should always be remembered, however, that a correlation between economic class and social sentiment carries no implication of unidirectional causality. Being a member of a certain class can mold a person's experiences and thus invigorate some sentiments more than others. But it is also true that holding particular sets of values and beliefs can stimulate or retard mobility. It sometimes happens, therefore, that people find themselves staying in or moving to particular strata because of the sentiments they previously held, instead of holding a given set of values owing to the class position they had earlier occupied.[17] We know that experiences and sentiments are related but we are not yet prepared to say how they are related.

It must also be remembered that history tends to record the actions, attitudes, and pronouncements of leaders with little regard for customs and beliefs of common people. But what we know of elites should not be imputed automatically to the masses.[18] Care should be taken on this point, for it is a methodological mistake social historians frequently make.

THIRD OBSERVATION: A CHANGE IN SENTIMENTS INFLUENCES THE COURSE OF HISTORY

History is an accumulation of actions and reactions. It is always important to remember that similar actions and events can have different consequences under varied conditions. Responses to the same event will vary according to popular sentiments. For instance, to "withhold freedom of thought from people who feel no need of it has no effect of any kind. To withhold it from people who do 'demand' it leaves desires unsated, so that they deepen in intensity."[19]

When the sentiment of combination dominates, people are able to interpret scripture liberally and remain flexible in adapting to the exigencies of the times. This societal condition tends to be compatible with cultural development and economic prosperity. But when the sentiment of group-persistence dominates, people are held to narrow and literal interpretations of doctrine.[20] This tends in some ways to obviate prospects for economic growth or scientific advancement. In this sense, too much conservatism can stand in the way of progress.[21] Stubborn adherence to tradition, reluctance to experiment or innovate, is frequently a formula for stagnation.

It is the blend of sentiments present in a society that influences the course of history.[22] A good balance is required if a society is to enjoy a maximization of social justice, economic prosperity, and cultural enrichment.[23] It must be pointed out that the balance of sentiments we speak of pertains to a mix of different kinds of people with different inclinations and proclivities. As one colloquial saying goes, it takes all kinds to make the world.

A homogeneous society might be imagined in which the requirement of uniformity would be the same in all individuals, and would correspond to the intermediate state just mentioned. But observation shows that that is not the case with human societies. Human societies are essentially heterogeneous, and the intermediate state is attained because the requirement of uniformity is very strong in some individuals, moderately strong in others, very feeble in still others, and almost entirely absent in a few. The average is found not in each individual, but in the group comprising them all.[24]

Every period is characterized by a certain amount of strain as the balance between these opposing inclinations shifts slightly in one direction or another.[25]

FOURTH OBSERVATION: HUMANS DESIRE RULES THAT ARE REASONABLE AND UNAMBIGUOUS

Every society faces an inescapable dilemma because human beings want to realize two different states of affairs that are irreconcilable. On the one hand, Pareto noted that all people want to live in a world where rules are reasonable and flexibly enforced. But people also want social conventions that provide unambiguous guidelines for behavior covering every situation in which they might find themselves. In other words, we want the freedom to act exactly as we please in a social world that is totally defined. This dilemma is a source of unrelenting tension. No society can maximize both conditions (freedom and constraint) simultaneously, so people will never be content for long. Broad discontent is eventually forged into a vague kind of consensus that there is too little freedom, or too much, too much ambiguity in the application of social conventions, or too little.[26]

The various elements of the social system undergo constant alteration, and an oscillating pattern of social change can be observed.[27] A major source of change develops when a gap between sentiments and experience becomes apparent. When social conventions fail to provide effective guidelines for behavior, either because they are too rigid to be consistent with the requirements of everyday life or because they are too equivocal to provide clear behavioral prescriptions, the incongruence between sentiments and experience creates a strain that can produce tumultuous change.[28] Recognizing this fact puts us squarely in a position to understand Pareto's theory of sentiment.

CYCLICAL DYNAMICS

Pareto viewed social change in terms of cyclical undulation between alternating periods when sentiments of combination first gain and then lose strength relative to the sentiments he called persistence of aggregates. In common parlance, periods of skepticism are followed by periods of faith, periods of liberalism are followed by periods of conservatism, periods of tolerance and receptivity to change are followed by periods of intolerance and stubborn adherence to tradition.

> Such developments may be described in other terms that emphasize one or another of their interesting aspects. Keeping to surfaces one may say that in history a period of faith will be followed by a period of skepticism, which will in turn be followed by another period of faith, this by another period of skepticism, and so on. . . . Looking a little deeper, one may say that society is grounded on group persistences. These manifest themselves in residues which, from the logico-experimental standpoint, are false, and sometimes patently absurd. When, therefore, the aspect of social utility predominates to any large extent, doctrines favourable to the sentiments of group-persistence are accepted, instinctively or otherwise. When, however, the logico-experimental aspect predominates, even to some slight extent, such doctrines are rejected and replaced by others that accord in appearance, though rarely in substance, with logico-experimental science. So the human mind oscillates between the two extremes, and being unable to halt at either, continues in movement indefinitely.[29]

We can look for evidence of shifts in sentiment in the events and doctrines of the past, and in actions and reactions that have been historically recorded. The popularity of Voltaire's work, for instance, represents something like a mountain of skepticism.[30]

It may be instructive to consider a relatively long period of time. Pareto traces changes in public sentiment in ancient Athens for a period of 150 years. The population as a whole was quite conservative and strong in persistence of aggregates at the time of the battles of Marathon (490 B.C.). But traditions rapidly declined in strength, as evidenced by Aeschylus' *Oresteia* (458 B.C.), a trilogy chronicling the defeat of those wishing to hold fast to tradition by those wanting to liberalize and encourage diversity and innovation. There was a brief period of reaction when the friends of Pericles were persecuted and Anaxagoras was forced to leave Athens (431 B.C.). But the literature of the ensuing period makes it clear that group persistences were losing strength. Consider the *Acharnians* (425 B.C.), the *Knights* (424 B.C.), and the *Clouds* (423 B.C.). All three comedies by Aristophanes indicate the rise of a new mode of thinking and the defeat of tradition. The old sense of values seems to have been thoroughly reduced by the time of Alcibiades and the Melos affair (416 B.C.), but we see a reaction when Alcibiades is chastised for profaning the mysteries (415 B.C.). The reaction is much in evidence by the time Socrates was prosecuted (399 B.C.) Sentiments seem relatively stable from then until the battle of Chaeroneia (338 B.C.) when Athens lost its independence and its history really blends with the history of the rest of Greece.[31]

A clear pattern of cyclical change emerges. And at least to Pareto's way of thinking, the social systemic strains that produced that pattern were equally clear.

> The fluctuations observable in social opinions result theoretically from a clash of two opposing forces: the correspondence of the derivations with reality on the one hand, and their social utility on the other. If the two things cogged together perfectly, a continuous movement ultimately leading to the absolute predominance of the resultant of the two forces would not be impossible; but since, instead of working in harmony, they are discordant, antagonistic, and since both a complete desertion of reality and a complete disregard of social utilities remain if not impossible, at least difficult, it necessarily follows that in regard to social matters theory oscillates like a pendulum, now swinging in one direction, now in the other.[32]

Now let us put Pareto's analysis in very plain language. There are times when traditional norms and values seem outmoded; when their strict application severely encumbers action and undermines convenient living, pursuit of happiness, or economic growth and prosperity. Under these conditions people are likely to feel that old ways should be flexibly interpreted, or sometimes changed, and that norms should be reasonably applied in light of varying circumstances. Faith in the old ways fades and traditions lose their grip. This trend continues in one direction until people come to the conclusion that too much has been lost. People get angry when there is a general feeling that too many values have been sacrificed in order to allow for individual freedom or in order to grant exceptions that have the effect of nullifying social convention. Under these circumstances every case can become an exception and rules have no meaning at all. It is then that a reaction sets in and people clamor for a reinvigoration of definitive norms and social constraint. "So there is no stopping, either, at the extreme where Class II residues predominate; and a new oscillation sets in heading back towards the first extreme, where Class I residues predominated. And so the pendulum continues swinging back and forth from one extreme to the other, indefinitely."[33]

The impact of economic exigencies on popular sentiment seems particularly striking. It seems clear that prosperity can gradually increase without having much impact on sentiments. But any truly rapid increase in wealth creates a very stark impression on people and seems to transform sentiments.[34] This is what happened in Rome, particularly within the elite.[35] This may also be what happened in Europe prior to the Reformation.[36] The observable pattern is for the increasing decadence of the ruling class to result in a sense of revulsion rising up from the less fortunate masses.

> Considered from the extrinsic standpoint, the Renaissance occurred in a period of economic prosperity. To that fact there is no end of testimony. It was also an age of rapid rise in prices, as the result of the inflow of precious metals from the Americas. Old institutions could no longer stand the strain. Everything seemed to need reforming. The modern world was being born. And then a religious reaction sets in and, as usual, it comes from the masses. Their leaders cared little about religion save as a tool of government. But for the masses it was the chief concern, and they tried their best to enforce it now in one way, now in another. It was the objective of many of their activities. The Reformation, in short, was one of the usual reactions by which Class II residues (group persistences) force a retreat upon Class I residues (the instinct for combinations).[37]

This description appears to bear some outward similarity with recent events in Iran, among other places. Another example presented itself with the first stirrings of the industrial revolution.

> The latter part of the eighteenth century was a period of economic prosperity. At that time we witness the first dawnings of modern transformations in agriculture, commerce, and industry. That circumstance favoured, as usual, a predominance of Class I residues, and was itself favoured by that predominance. The tide of economic prosperity rose first in England, and that is why the curve for Class II residues, as regards their relative proportions to Class I residues, first shows a drop in that country; and that also is why, in virtue of the undulating movement peculiar to that curve, even with economic conditions remaining virtually

constant, England was the first country to experience a reaction toward a
rise in the curve. So, both the action and reaction in England anticipated
the corresponding movements in France. The action was 'philosophic' in
outward garb in both countries; the reaction, though substantially the
same, assumed different forms, being Christian in England and democratic in France. The French Revolution was a religious reaction of the
same type, under a different form, as the religious reaction in England,
and also of the same type as the religious reaction represented by the
Reformation. But it was soon to change its costume. Democratic and
humanitarian in the early stages of the Revolution, it became patriotic
and belligerent under Napoleon, then Catholic under Louis XVIII. The
high point in the curve of the relative preponderance of Class II over Class
I residues was reached, taking Europe as a whole, shortly after 1815; and
the exteriors everywhere were Christian.[38]

PARETO'S THEORY OF SENTIMENT

Pareto presents his readers with the broad outlines of a theory of
sentiment. "We have time and time again been led to recognize that one
of the principal factors determining the social equilibrium was the
relative proportions of Class I and Class II residues in individuals."[39]
The course of history is both marked and channeled by these recurring
cycles between faith and skepticism. Periods of faith are generally
characterized by high levels of conformity to clear and precise behavioral conventions, and during periods of skepticism, social conventions
are less clear and the nature and conditions for their application are
more likely to be open to debate. Conformity declines correspondingly.[40]
    The problem lies in the tension between sentiments of combination
and persistence of aggregates. Owing to sentiments of "combination,"
people want the freedom to experiment and to respond flexibly to
situations. But they also crave clear rules that unambiguously specify
appropriate behavior. Owing to sentiments of "persistence of aggregates," people want tradition and some level of conformity. But the
more consensus there is that rules are irrational or too rigid, the more
likely sentiments of combination are to gain strength and sentiments of
group persistence are to recede. This legitimates nonconformist behavior, questioning of authority, and social experimentation.
    Over time, popular demand for freedom results in a general
relaxation of social control that has deleterious consequences. The more
consensus there is that rules are too lax and that people are too free, then

the more likely sentiments of group persistence are to gain strength and sentiments of combination are to recede.[41] Of course, people's perceptions about rigidity or laxity of social proscriptions will be formed in response to the ongoing flow of political and economic events. We can capture Pareto's insights about cyclical change in a series of succinct propositions.[42]

Observers have long noted that popular mood and social values seem to move through cycles of liberalism and conservatism, faith and skepticism. But Pareto does more than repeat old adages and mirror the generalizations of others. He implicitly suggests a theoretical explanation for the changes that take place. Translated into a series of succinct propositions, Pareto's explanation of the dynamics of social sentiment should enable us to predict how much change will occur in a given direction, when a reversal will occur, and how substantial the reaction in the opposite direction will be.

Of course, we know that economic trends and political events have a significant impact on social sentiment. For instance, with increased prosperity, Class I sentiments tend to replace Class II sentiments. Art, literature, science, and philosophy blossom and flourish, while religion, nationalism, and tradition tend to subside.[43] It is in this sense that analysis of sentiments becomes quite complex. Social sentiment has many different dimensions and so touches many aspects of culture, social structure, and social life.[44] As these principles suggest, a reaction can set in, often manifesting itself in political repression or reduced freedom of expression. Pornography can be a good indicator of social change because it is more likely to be tolerated during periods of general prosperity, receptivity to change, and tolerance of diversity, than during periods of stubborn adherence to tradition when it is viewed by conservative elements as a symbol of decadence or the embodiment of evil. Hence, the degree to which sexual expression is tolerated or persecuted serves as a good indicator of shifts in popular sentiment of all kinds.[45]

Major historical trends suddenly take on a whole new meaning when we keep Pareto's theory of sentiment in mind. What was the "authoritarian personality" of the 1930s and 1940s, if not a person who, disturbed by the cultural decadence and disillusioned by the economic hardships of the late 1920s and early 1930s, concluded it was time for the introduction and enforcement of more rigid rules governing people's lives? And who were the people of the "me generation" if not individuals who, being raised in a period of rather rigid conformity, rapid social

TABLE 7.1
An Elementary Theory of Social Sentiment

(1)	The more equivocal norms become (6), then (1) the less constrained people are in their behavior and the more likely actions of potential but unproven deteriment to others are to be tolerated.
(2)	The less constraining norms are and the more tolerant people are of actions of potential but unproven detriment (1), then (2) the more confusion there is likely to be over definitions of appropriate behavior and the more likely people are to be injured or offended by the imprudent actions of others.
(3)	The more confusion there is over definitions of appropriate behavior and the more injury and offense people sustain due to the imprudent actions of others (2), then (3) the more likely people are to seek coherent traditions and unequivocal prescriptions.
(4)	The less equivocal prescriptions become (3), then (4) the more constrained people are and the more likely people are to fear being blamed for the anticipated and unanticipated consequences of their actions.
(5)	The more constraining norms are and the more inhibited people are out of fear of blame (4), then (5) the more likely people are to question the rationality of normative beliefs and the more likely people are to avoid helping others.
(6)	The more people question the rationality of beliefs and the more hesitant people are to cooperate with others (5), then (6) the more likely they are to seek relaxed prescriptions and freedom of autonomous action.

change, and unbounded economic opportunity, concluded that rules should be waived unless their application can be justified on a case-by-case basis? The natural question to ask now is, what is next? People seeking an answer to that question have only to consider contemporary events in light of the inventory of propositions presented in Table 7.1.

The important point to hammer home is that informative and illuminating theoretical principles are suggested by Pareto's argument. These principles offer a compelling explanation for the cyclical shifts in social sentiment observable throughout history. These are the core of Pareto's theoretical framework.

In this chapter, we have presented a propositional formulation of Pareto's elementary theory of social sentiment. Pareto also had elementary theories of economy and politics and those will be presented in the chapters that follow. Pareto paid close attention to ways in which sentiment, economy, and political organization influence one another. These linkages unify his three elementary theories into a single "general sociology." We will pay closer attention to these linkages in the chapters that follow. For the time being, it should be noted that the elementary theory of sentiments presented in this chapter is the core of Pareto's general sociology.

NOTES

1. Vilfredo Pareto, *The Transformation of Democracy*, ed. Charles Powers (R. Girola, trans.) (New Brunswick, NJ: Transaction Books, 1984); originally published in 1921.

2. Charles Powers, "Pareto's Theory of Society," *Revue européenne des science sociales et cahiers Vilfredo Pareto* 19, (1981) 59: 99-119.

3. Vilfredo Pareto, *The Mind and Society* (hereafter, *Treatise*), ed. A. Livingston (A. Bongiorno and A. Livingston with J. H. Rogers, trans.) (New York: Harcourt Brace Jovanovich, 1935); reprinted by Dover Press in 1963 and AMS in 1983 under the original 1916 title, *Treatise on General Sociology*.

4. Ibid., section 1690.

5. Ibid., section 1690, footnote 1.

6. Pareto, *The Transformation of Democracy*, p. 63.

7. Vilfredo Pareto, *The Rise and Fall of the Elites*, introduced by Hans Zetterberg (Totowa, NJ: Bedminster, 1968); originally published in 1901.

8. Pareto, *Treatise*, section 1731.

9. Ibid., section 1732.

10. Ibid., section 1721.

11. Ibid., chapter 11.

12. Ibid., section 1680.

13. Ibid., section 1681.

14. Charles Powers and Robert Hanneman, "Pareto's Theory of Social Cycles: A Formal Model and Simulation," *Sociological Theory* 1 (1983): 59-89.

15. Pareto, *Treatise*, section 1839.

16. Ibid., section 1723.

17. Ibid., section 1732.

18. Ibid., section 1734.

19. Ibid., section 1753.

20. Ibid., section 1800.

21. Ibid., section 1806.

22. Ibid., section 2155.

23. Ibid., section 2171.

24. Ibid., section 2172.

25. Ibid., section 2173.

26. Ibid., sections 1256-1383.

27. Ibid., section 2338.

28. Ibid., section 2339.

29. Ibid., section 2341.

30. Ibid., section 2344.

31. Ibid., section 2345.

32. Ibid., section 1683.

33. Ibid., section 2340.

34. Ibid., section 2351.

35. Ibid., section 2354.

36. Ibid., section 2375-2377.

37. Ibid., section 2384.

38. Ibid., section 2386.

39. Ibid., section 2413.

40. Ibid., sections 1256-1383.

41. Ibid., sections 1111-1113 and 1660 ff.

42. This table represents an improvement upon past work. See Powers, *Pareto's Theory*, p. 109. Pareto is explicit on certain points. When norms relax, some people begin behaving unacceptably and a reaction sets in. But when norms tighten, people eventually come to resent the lack of freedom and an opposite reaction sets in. The other points contained in Table 7.1 are far more oblique and hidden in Pareto's work. In a sense they are being read into Pareto by Powers.

43. Pareto, *Treatise*, section 2513.

44. Pareto, *Transformation*.

45. Pareto, *Treatise*, section 2521.

8

Toward a Sociological Theory of Economy

In order to understand Pareto's development as a theorist, it is important to remember that he turned to sociology because of questions he was unable to answer as an economist. Pareto held the conviction that economic phenomena can only be understood within a broad historical and sociopolitical context. His answer to the intellectual problems confronting economists was to develop a "general sociology." His theory of undulating change in popular sentiment (Chapter 7) is at the core of this "general sociology."

Once Pareto had accounted, at least to his own satisfaction, for those cyclical shifts in sentiment that seem to characterize the passage of history, he was ready to advance an economic theory within the rubric of his "general sociology."[1] He argued that social dynamics produce aggregate changes in the propensities to work, save, and consume. These, in turn, are responsible for infrastructural transformations in the economy because entrepreneurs modify their investment strategies in light of shifting tastes and demands. Such infrastructural changes influence prospects for sustained economic growth.

ON ECONOMIC BEHAVIOR

Pareto began his career as a conventional economist. Without assuming rationality on the part of economic actors, he nonetheless focused on patterns of supply and demand.

> Individuals and communities are spurred by instinct and reason to acquire possession of material goods that are useful—or merely pleasurable—for purposes of living, as well as to seek consideration and honours. Such impulses, which may be called "interests," play in the mass a very important part in determining the social equilibrium.[2]

On an abstract level, focusing on tastes and obstacles enables us to think about important economic functions (like productivity) as equilibrium points. But there is no inherent economic tendency toward optimal outcomes or maximum utility. To presume that there is involves an error in reasoning. We cannot assume optimal economic states for a society at large because communities are composed of different kinds of people with a diversity of needs and desires. Individuals usually do what they believe is best for themselves and their families, and not necessarily what is in the national interest.[3] The problem is that the aggregation of consequences of independent actions can be quite inconsistent with the goals of the individual as well as the best interests of the society. Family planning is a perfect example. In many parts of the world, people have large families because children are regarded as a commercial asset and a family with many children has more security than a family with few children. Consequently, people desire large families. But if most people have many children, the average family will acquire less than it would if most people had few children because population increase is associated with resource scarcity. India is a case in point. It has immense natural and human resources and would be a rich country were its population equal in number to that of the United States instead of three times the size of the U.S. population. The overall effect of everyone pursuing an individual policy of having more children in order to acquire more wealth is that the society can impoverish itself and the average person ends up materially worse off. "Free market" solutions do not automatically result in the greatest good for the greatest number.[4]

Simply saying that people act according to tastes and obstacles, or by balancing off what they want against the costs involved in getting what they want, tells us very little and does not take us at all far in our efforts to account for societal change. Pareto urged readers to remember that economic behavior, like everything else, has its rudimentary base in instinct and sentiment. Entrepreneurs tend to be strong in combinations, whereas people who save tend to be strong in persistence of aggregates. That is why, he maintained, entrepreneurs are generally adventurous and savers rather staid.[5] The entrepreneur, endowed with special skills, is able to turn adverse circumstances to his or her own benefit. This often results in even higher profits and sometimes higher productivity. But frugal people who work hard and save are the backbone of a healthy economy. Hence, it takes all kinds of people in order to stimulate and maintain economic growth.[6] Shifts in social sentiment have a very significant impact on economic trends.

This complicates matters greatly and necessitates that a theory of sentiments be infused into any analysis of the economy in order to account for the factors that have paramount effect on economic trends: namely, the relative propensities to work, loaf, save, consume, waste, or invest. Shifts in social sentiment have a very direct effect on these factors and can thereby either fuel or impede, stimulate or retard current economic trends.[7]

PARETO'S EARLY ECONOMIC MODEL

Like most economists of his day, one of Pareto's principal concerns was with the business cycle. No matter how positive an economic forecast is, expansion cannot be maintained indefinitely. By the same token, no matter how dire conditions become, economic depression is in reality a temporary state. Periods of expansion and contraction follow one another in succession. The most formidable periods of economic expansion can take root in the very depths of severe depressions when stagnation seems inescapable. And the most devastating depressions can follow periods of almost unprecedented prosperity when self-sustained growth seems assured. This led Pareto to conclude that depression actually creates the conditions necessary for growth, whereas prosperity undermines those conditions.

Pareto's initial explanation of economic and business cycles focuses on the availability of capital and is more economic than sociological.[8] It takes a great deal of investment to spur periods of economic expansion. But massive investment tends to deplete the reservoir of savings available for future investment, thus precipitating a period of decline. Investment activity remains low during the initial stages of economic contraction, in part because of capital scarcity and in part because investment entails substantial risk during initial periods of contraction when economic conditions seem to get worse day by day. But the more prolonged the downturn the more opportunity there is for the reservoir of capital to replenish itself. This supply of investment capital provides the primary ingredient for expansion, especially when a downturn seems to bottom out, thus reducing the risks associated with new investment.

Pareto added to this basic framework with a rather sophisticated analysis. He argued that: (1) General prosperity enables people to satisfy tastes for unnecessary consumer goods and services. (2) Capitalists respond to growing demand for consumer goods and services by investing in the consumer sector rather than the capital-producing sector. (3) Economic growth in general means that there is a larger infrastructure to maintain. Greater depreciation and replacement costs are therefore involved just to maintain the growing volume of economic activity. And (4) consumer goods and service industries can tend to have particularly high depreciation and replacement needs, at least in part because of the stress consumers place on fads and newness. As a consequence of all these factors, the level of replacement costs required to maintain the status quo is especially great in a prosperous, consumer-oriented economy. Therefore, the more prosperous and the more consumer oriented the economy, the more difficult it is to produce capital in excess of basic replacement needs, unless there is some external windfall such as Roman extraction of taxes from the provinces, Spanish removal of gold and silver from the Americas, or the increased flow of petrodollars to OPEC countries after 1973. But there are no windfalls for most societies. So the greater the level of prosperity and the greater the corresponding investment of energy in consumer-oriented sectors of the economy, the more difficult it is to maintain the level of investment necessary to sustain growth.[9]

There is not much impetus to invest during periods of economic downturn. Investment in the consumer-oriented sectors is particularly unattractive because it makes little sense to build establishments catering to people who have no money in their pockets. This is why a general economic decline can be especially disastrous for businesses in consumer sectors.

Severe contraction in consumer sectors has two indirect consequences. First, the level of investment needed to sustain the economy

TABLE 8.1
An Elementary Theory of Economy

(1) The greater the availability of capital and will to invest (6), then (1) the more probable that economic expansion becomes.

(2) The greater the increase in productivity (1), then (2) the greater the expansion of consumer-oriented sectors of the economy relative to capital-producing sectors.

(3) The larger the economy (1) and the lower the relative commitment of resources to production of capital (2), then (3) the greater the replacement needs resulting from depreciation, the greater the probability of capital shortages, and the more hesitant people will be (as a result of high interest rates) to invest in the expansion of industry.

(4) The more serious that capital shortages become and the more hesitant people are to invest in expansion of basic industries (3), then (4) the more probable that economic contraction becomes.

(5) The more productivity declines (4), then (5) the greater the decline of consumer-oriented sectors relative to capital-producing sectors of the economy.

(6) The smaller the economy and the greater the relative commitment of resources to the production of capital (5), then (6) the lower the replacement needs resulting from depreciation, the greater the availability of capital, and the less hesitant people will be to invest in economic expansion.

diminishes because there is a smaller physical plant to maintain and because the sector with the higher rate of depreciation experiences the most severe dislocation. Second, the production of capital expands, at least relative to the size and investment needs of the economy, due to increasing importance of the capital-producing sector relative to the consumer products and services sectors. These trends produce a reservoir of excess capital that can be used to fuel future economic growth. Pareto's analysis can be translated into a series of succinct propositions.[10]

Here again, we see the genius for which Pareto was so famous. By focusing on the consequences and reverberations of one set of changes for the overall economy, Pareto was able to reveal ways that movement in one direction produce countervailing forces that eventually reverse the original trend. Prosperity is not self-sustaining. Neither is depression inescapable. Economic cycles occur because prosperity destroys the very conditions on which it is predicated and economic decline creates the very conditions that spur growth.

MULTIPLIER AND ACCELERATOR EFFECTS

Pareto's economic analysis bears a great deal in common with contemporary analyses of multiplier and accelerator effects.[11] Entrepreneurs are encouraged to increase their investments during periods when economic growth seems assured and profits seem secure. Greater net investment, or investment in excess of depreciation and replacement costs, means that people must be employed to build, operate, and maintain new facilities. This is the "accelerator" effect in action. The "multiplier" effect takes hold when those newly employed people make a further contribution to general prosperity by spending their wages on consumer items. So increased impetus to invest stimulates the economy in two different ways.

Pareto would also argue that the accelerator and multiplier effects can operate to dampen economic activity. Not all contemporary economists would agree with this position, but the argument is nonetheless plausible. When consumer spending stops growing, there is a tendency for entrepreneurs to stop investing in new facilities. A slowdown in construction translates into layoffs by way of the deceleration effect. And layoffs mean reduced consumer expenditures via reverse operation of the multiplier effect. Hence, a mere reduction in the rate of economic growth, not even an actual economic decline but simply a reduction in the rate of growth, could conceivably tailspin into a recession as new construction is cut back, resulting in reduced consumer expenditures, leading to further cutbacks in construction, producing still further reductions in consumer outlay.

Pareto suggested, and contemporary research seems to bear out, that elasticity in saving, credit buying, and the consumption of consumer durables are particularly important in this process. The Great Depression can be analyzed in just these terms. There was a marked increase in consumer spending and credit buying throughout the 1920s. The explosion in consumer spending centered on durable goods like ice boxes and automobiles. This is a rather crucial point and deserves special notice. A great many consumer goods and services are relatively inelastic. Come good times or bad, consumption is relatively stable. Cigarette sales are an example. Fluctuations do occur in tobacco consumption but they are not clearly related to the business cycle. Some people smoke less during bad times in an effort to save money. But other people smoke more as a nervous reaction to the problems, tensions, and uncertainties the recession brings.

In contrast, consumer durables are highly elastic. When times are good and people feel optimistic enough about the future to deplete their savings or incur debt, they spend comparatively large sums of money on cars, washing machines, and the like. But when times are hard or when people regard the future as insecure or feel too pessimistic to deplete savings or incur debt, purchases of consumer durables plummet. And inactivity in the consumer durables industries then reverberates throughout the economy. Reduced cigarette sales hurt tobacco farmers, but reduced automobile sales are felt in the steel, rubber, plastics, electronics, glass, paint, and petroleum industries.

During good times, there is a tendency for people to begin by depleting savings and end by incurring debt in order to finance the purchase of consumer durable goods. This fuels further economic growth. The production of durable goods means expansion of heavy industries that provide basic materials (e.g., steel), as well as factories for manufacturing and assembly, and firms for distribution and servicing. But there is great risk in an expansion fueled by credit buying, for there can come a time when consumers are, on the whole, overextended. Tightening credit means that consumption declines because people are no longer allowed to live beyond their means. The consumer durables market is the first to feel the effect of reductions in buying power. People who reach their credit limits still have to eat but are usually able to get along without a new car. Reduced sales of consumer durables means less demand for steel, rubber, and other basic commodities. All this translates into lost jobs, which means further reductions in consumer expenditures, as people who have fallen on hard times struggle to service those debts they incurred during the previous expansionary and credit buying period. The result is an economic "crash dive." The very consumer borrowing and spending patterns that produced the "New Era Prosperity" of the 1920s seem to have created the preconditions for the Great Depression.[12]

The opposite dynamics take hold on an economic down cycle. The Great Depression turned most people, or at least those old enough at the time to have really experienced its horrors, into frugal pessimists. Inclined to save and wary of accumulating debts, these citizens provided the backbone for economic recovery in the 1950s. They were hard working, willing to give honest value for a reasonable wage, and through their collective frugality provided a reservoir of savings that enabled economic takeoff.

Although most economists recognize the importance of elasticity in patterns of consumer saving and spending, the dynamics of frugality, consumption, saving, and credit buying are largely sociological rather than economic. Pareto made an important contribution to economics by suggesting a general sociological framework within which economic phenomena might be studied. He provides us with a sociological explanation for events that have great impact on the economy. Popular sentiment changes with the times. When self-centered pursuit of gratification seems legitimate, the propensity to save diminishes and credit buying and conspicuous consumption increase. This occurs because of the sociological dynamics described in the last chapter. Economic prosperity is at first stimulated and then eventually undermined by the operation of these processes.

SOCIAL DETERMINANTS OF ECONOMIC CYCLES

Pareto turned his attention to sociology because he was convinced that this was the only way to develop an adequate understanding of economic cycles. This follows from his assumption that societies are "social systems" composed of interdependent parts. Economic events influence, and in turn are influenced by, popular sentiment. It is for this reason that his theory of "general sociology" is designed to subsume and integrate the studies of popular sentiment, economic cycles, and political organization. The theory was initially advanced in *The Rise and Fall of the Elites*,[13] developed in *Treatise on General Sociology*,[14] and refined, clarified, and applied in *The Transformation of Democracy*.[15]

The starting point for Pareto's general sociology is his elementary theory of sentiment, presented in Chapter 7. People seek beliefs that are both useful and realistic. Norms that are overly constraining strike people as being unrealistic guides for everyday behavior. There is a clear tendency to move toward more relaxed proscriptions when citizens reach an implicit consensus that rules are too inflexible, unrealistic, and overly constraining. On aggregate, people appreciate this change, the popular mood in favor of liberalization solidifies, and the trend toward relaxation of proscriptions gains momentum. This tends to be particularly true in times of general economic or technological change, because economic expansion and technological development have a way of placing people in new circumstances and new situations where the applicability of old rules seems imperfect. People press outward against all the old social conventions and boundaries of permissibility. Moreover, when rules are generally thought to be too restrictive, any challenge against existing norms tends to have a certain amount of legitimacy deriving from the prevailing climate of permissiveness.

The problem is that challenges to convention grow in audacity as the defense of tradition diminishes. Relaxation of social constraint gives rise to disagreements concerning the boundary between acceptable and unacceptable behavior. Furthermore, no person enjoys meaningful protection in a society where every person thinks anything is permissible. Actions in utter disregard for the interests of others become more flagrant and people begin to clamor for more restrictive social proscriptions. Social sentiments change and constraint increases. People are then pleased with more stringent proscriptions and greater firmness in the enforcement of rules. Public sentiment hardens and the trend toward greater social constraint gains momentum. But it is only a matter of time before social constraint generates resistance and a reversal in the trend.

Pareto's elementary theory of sentiment has been propositionally stated (see Table 1, Chapter 7) and suggests the dynamic process of change in public mood. But it is Pareto's theory of "general sociology" that focuses on the linkages among his elementary theories of sentiment (Chapter 7), economy (beginning of Chapter 8), and political organization (beginning of Chapter 9). Because public sentiment, economic productivity, and political organization are presumed to influence one another, trends on one cycle can be adequately understood and predicted only by taking account of changes on the other cycles as well. In this section, we will explore Pareto's analysis of the linkage between public sentiment and economic productivity.

Pareto based his analysis on the assumption that people are driven by deep-seated value orientations, and his use of the scheme to analyze events in Italy around 1920 is instructive. Pareto's portrayal of Italy is by no means altogether fair or fully accurate. It is of interest for the theoretical hypotheses it yields rather than the characterization of Italy itself. Pareto argued that people had developed a penchant for squandering the resources of others. Rather than trying to work hard and build something for themselves, the dominant social sentiments of the times encouraged people to seek their fortune through speculation, connivance, or largess. Everyone wanted something for nothing. Capitalists wanted monopoly rights and protective tariffs so that they could be assured of selling inferior products at high prices. Workers wanted high wages and guaranteed job security so that they could be assured of a good standard of living regardless of work performance. The rich and privileged wanted preferential treatment so that they could be assured of maintaining their positions without regard to work or level of competence. The peasants wanted land or guaranteed wage employment as protection against insecurity. And the urban proletariat wanted social welfare benefits that would guarantee a decent standard of living for all, regardless of employment status. Everyone wanted more. Such a society, Pareto argued, can never sustain prosperity because it impoverishes itself.[16] In this sense, economic trends are contingent upon social sentiment.[17]

> These crises resulted not only from strictly economic causes, but were also determined by human nature; and further, that they were only one of many manifestations of the psychological rhythm. In other words as I just stated, there is a rhythm of sentiment which we can observe in ethics. . .[18]

Sustaining growth requires that people are willing to work hard and delay gratification. A society that glorifies hard work, universal responsibility, professional commitment, and frugality is a society that will enjoy future prosperity. This fact is epitomized by experiences in Western Europe[19] and by the economic miracle of Japan in the decades following World War II.[20] But when popular beliefs legitimize self-gratification, evasion of responsibility, and avoidance of work, the aggregate effect is to sap economic potential and undermine economic performance.[21]

What, then, are the linkages between sentiment and productivity? Pareto asserts that every society periodically enters eras when ethical standards and normative constraints become more relaxed (Chapter 7). Economic expansion stimulates the trend toward relaxation of normative proscriptions because economic growth tends to create new opportunities that are trying on old norms. And a general trend toward relaxation of norms tends to legitimize the pursuit of self-gratification, for as the social climate becomes less restrictive people lose their inhibitions and become more hedonistic. This has important economic consequences. Hedonistic people are less inclined to save and are more free to spend money—even if this means borrowed money—on consumer delights, conspicuous consumption, and the gratification of wants. This kind of behavior is encouraged and legitimated in economically prosperous societies where advertisers constantly create new demands for the latest styles, fashions, and fads. People are taught that it is normal to want things (or experiences) and admirable to indulge those wants. As if to further legitimize hedonism, there are historical periods when citizens heap reward, deference, and esteem on those who are most stylish and most successful in the pursuit of self-satisfaction.

All the borrowing and spending that results further accelerates economic growth, and this acceleration stimulates still greater relaxation of norms.

Reducing social constraint and glorifying the pursuit of self-gratification also has a second set of economic implications. It encourages people to be more "creative" in devising occupations. Speculation and parasitic activities abound. Perhaps the most insidious parasitic activities involve the proliferation of needless paperwork in order to create more legal sector and government employment. The danger is that a society can be strangled under the weight of an extensive legal apparatus or a suspicious and overbearing bureaucracy that does not want or will not tolerate entrepreneurial innovation.

Very important shifts in economic infrastructure occur as a result of these tendencies. It seemed to Pareto that speculation and parasitic professions gain in importance when social proscriptions are relaxed. Moreover, people borrow and consume when self-gratification is encouraged by popular beliefs. The economy enjoys hearty expansion, fueled especially by improved sales of consumer durables. A prolonged expansion of this type can produce significant modifications in the economic infrastructure as investors seek to exploit growing demand for consumer goods and services.

But the further that trends continue in this direction the more likely a reversal is and the more dramatic the reversal is inclined to be.[22] Consumers who have learned to want a great deal of gratification are likely to develop bleak outlooks once they have exhausted savings and accumulated big debts. This shift in popular sentiment undermines consumer confidence and, at least in Pareto's estimation, discourages conspicuous consumption. The aggregate result of more frugal consumer behavior can be economic contraction, which further undermines consumer confidence and fosters conservative outlooks. This, of course, is not all bad. Conservative people tend to work hard and save. Their efforts generate the impetus for the next round of economic expansion. "In periods of economic stagnancy there is an increase in the quantity of available savings, and that is the groundwork for the ensuing 'boom' when the amount of available savings will diminish and so open the way to another period of stagnancy. And so on indefinitely."[23] The descriptions Pareto provided allow us to specify a series of propositions about feedback mechanisms linking his elementary theory of sentiment with his elementary theory of economy.[24] These feedback mechanisms constitute the first of three parts to Pareto's "general sociology" linking cycles of sentiment, economic productivity, and political organization.

TABLE 8.2   General Sociology Part I: Dynamics Linking
Public Sentiment and Economic Productivity

(1) The greater the rate of increase in productivity (6), then (1) the more likely it is that increasing complexity and opportunity in life will bring traditional beliefs into conflict with actual experiences, with the result that there will be increased pressure for relaxation of social prescriptions.

(2) The more relaxed social prescriptions become (1), then (2) the more legitimate self-gratification becomes, thus encouraging a consumer-based economic boom and infrastructural transformation to a consumer-oriented economy.

(3) The greater the levels of consumer debt and infrastructural transformation to a consumer-oriented economy (2), then (3) the more scarce unutilized capital becomes and the more likely the economy is to contract.

(4) The greater the level of economic contraction (3), then (4) the greater the shortfall between aspirations and socioeconomic attainment, and the more restrictive social prescriptions are likely to become.

(5) The more constraining social prescriptions are (4), then (5) the less legitimate it will be to pursue self-gratification so that consumer spending diminishes, consumer-oriented industries are undermined, and the aggregate level of savings begins to increase.

(6) The greater the level of infrastructural transformation to a capital-producing economy and the greater the accumulation of private savings (5), then (6) the greater the reservoir of excess capital available for investment and the more likely a business-led economic recovery becomes.

Hence, the operation of the economic cycles is inherently tied to the operation of cycles in popular sentiment. One set of public values retards consumer consumption but creates the conditions for a business-led recovery. The prosperity associated with a business-led recovery then transforms values. These new values provide the impetus for a consumer-led boom but also undermine the foundations that economic prosperity rests upon. Values are transformed again in the depressionary period that must inexorably follow. This value transformation precludes the possibility of a consumer-led boom but creates, over time, some of the necessary conditions for a business-led recovery.

Economic expansion tends to encourage relaxation in social proscriptions, which in turn stimulates still more short-term economic growth and expansion. But shift in public sentiment also generates changes in the basic economic infrastructure. A consumer-oriented society has an ever growing need for reinvestment to replace old equipment and material, and also has an ever expanding need to create demand for new products and services. Yet, such societies have more capacity to create demand than to generate and distribute the wealth needed to satisfy that demand. They divest energy (at least in relative terms) away from capital producing industries, and at the same time allow consumer debt to balloon.

Thus it is that the same shifts in popular sentiment that help to fuel short-term economic growth (by increasing demand) also simultaneously create the conditions for economic decline (by depleting savings). Once contraction sets in people tend to realize they have been living beyond their means and, it might be added, a conservative reaction gains momentum. New found conservatism is often forcefully imposed by lending agencies that will no longer extend aggregate consumer credit. Diminished consumer spending, in turn, undermines economic expansion and sets recessionary processes in motion. The gathering storm of recession further fuels the tendency toward conservatism in popular mood. Unnecessary consumption is restricted, the consumer sector declines, and the depression worsens. But as the economy contracts, the need for replacement capital diminishes and a reservoir of personal savings tends to accumulate. These factors provide the necessary ingredients for a subsequent period of expansion.[25]

POLITICAL DETERMINANTS OF ECONOMIC CYCLES

Pareto argued that economic cycles also respond to changes in political climate, and these merit brief mention as a prelude to Chapter 9. Some regimes try to maintain their power by co-opting powerful interest groups. In fact, Pareto argued that this is the common fate of most democracies. They are transformed into plutocracies, or governments by the wealthy, because great numbers of people are complacent about corruption and inefficiency as long as a few crumbs are disbursed in their direction. Regimes commonly extend social welfare benefits, subsidize prices, and provide large numbers of patronage jobs in order to keep common people satisfied, at the same time using government contracts, protective tariffs, and prestigious government positions in order to placate the rich. This kind of demagogic plutocracy, de facto rule by the rich with de jure rule by the masses, can result in horrible government. The interests of the regime are promoted at the expense of economic efficiency and the greatest good for the greatest number, a fact that not infrequently bankrupts a society (see Chapter 9).

IMPLICATIONS

Pareto's work suggests a penetrating and informative analysis of industrial economies. Economic growth can be stimulated or retarded by changing patterns in consumer spending. But the two truly interesting questions, the questions traditional economists tend to avoid but that Pareto tried to answer, are the following: (1) Why do undulating shifts tend to occur in public sentiment? (2) How are those shifts in popular sentiment related to structural dynamics in the economy? He presents us with a sociological explanation for cyclical oscillation in sentiment (Chapter 7), which enables us to understand better the sociological dynamics underlying economic change (Chapter 8). The synchronization of these economic and sociological cycles is thus revealed.[26]

Pareto presents us with a starkly radical theory of economy. In his view, economic activity is not the same as productive activity. Economies that are geared toward speculation, patronage, wasteful militarization, or conspicuous consumption cannot be expected to sustain prosperity. Shifts in public sentiment away from stubborn adherence to established ways and toward cunning, deceit, and wile, stimulate economic growth in the short term but also undermine basic industry, deplete the society's reservoir of accumulated savings, and destroy the work ethic. This transformation detracts from long-term economic potential.

NOTES

1. This chapter is based largely upon Charles Powers's previously published article, "Sociopolitical Determinants of Economic Cycles: Vilfredo Pareto's Final Statement," *Social Science Quarterly* 65, 4 (1984): 988-1001.

2. Vilfredo Pareto, *The Mind and Society* (hereafter, *Treatise*) Section 2009, ed. Arthur Livingston (A. Bongiorno and A. Livingston with J. H. Rogers, trans.) (New York: Harcourt Brace Jovanovich, 1935); reprinted by Dover in 1963 and AMS in 1983 under the original 1916 title, *Treatise on General Sociology*.

3. Ibid., sections 2115-2138.

4. On the other hand, protectionism sometimes works. There are so many factors to consider that one cannot conclude, a priori, that protectionism will destroy national wealth. Pareto, *Treatise*, section 2217.

5. Ibid., section 2316.

6. Ibid., sections 2216, 2254.

7. Ibid., section 2013.

8. Vilfredo Pareto, *Manual of Political Economy*, ed. Ann Schwier and Alfred Page (A. Schwier, trans.) (New York: August M. Kelley, 1971); translated from the second edition that was originally published in 1909.

9. Ibid, chapter 3.

10. Powers, *Pareto's Final Statement*.

11. For instance, see Paul Samuelson, *Economics* (New York: McGraw-Hill, 1980).

12. For instance, see Frederic Miskin, "The Household Balance-Sheet and the Great Depression." *Journal of Economic History* 38 (1978): 918-937.

13. Vilfredo Pareto, *The Rise and Fall of the Elites*, introduced by Hans Zetterberg (Totowa, NJ: Bedminster, 1968); originally published in 1901.

14. Pareto, *Treatise*.

15. Vilfredo Pareto, *The Transformation of Democracy*, ed. Charles Powers (R. Girola, trans.) (New Brunswick, NJ: Transaction Books, 1984); originally published in 1921.

16. Ibid., chapter 4.

17. Pareto, *Treatise*, section 2097.

18. Pareto, *Elites*, pp. 30-31.

19. For example, see Max Weber, *General Economic History*, introduced by Ira Cohen (F. Knight, trans.) (New Brunswick, NJ: Transaction Books, 1982); originally published in 1923.

20. See, for example, Ezra Vogel, *Modern Japanese Organization* (Berkeley: University of California Press, 1985).

21. Pareto, *Transformation*.

22. Pareto, *Treatise*, section 2311-2312.

23. Ibid., section 2318.

24. These principles are an improved version of those presented in Charles Powers, "Pareto's Theory of Society," *Revue europeene des sciences sociales et cahiers Vilfredo Pareto* 19, 59 (1981): 99-119.

25. Pareto, *Treatise*, section 2311-2312

26. Ibid., sections 2293-2294.

9

Toward a Sociological Theory of Politics

For most of his life, Pareto argued that political change takes form in the replacement of one set of leaders by another. This was his famous theory of "circulation of elites." He posited that the longer a regime is in power, the more decadent rulers become and the less skillful or adept they are in the strategic use of force. As leaders become more decadent, they extract a greater and greater portion of the national wealth for their own use, thus inciting jealousy and fomenting discontent. But at the very time they exploit more in order to satisfy their growing taste for luxury, they also become less adept in the art of social control, and therefore less capable of defending their privileged positions against growing opposition. Regimes change when decadent rulers succumb to opposition movements led by people who have less taste for luxury and are more proficient in the willful use of naked force.

Pareto's analysis borrows heavily from Machiavelli, and this theory of "circulation of elites" has gained considerable popularity.[1] It is the theory for which Pareto is best remembered by most sociologists. The only problem is that Pareto, without going so far as to disavow the theory of "circulation of elites," subsumed it within the rubric of a different analysis of politics in his final monograph. Unfortunately, *The*

Transformation of Democracy (1921) has been largely ignored by scholars and was not even translated into English until 1984.[2] Perhaps Pareto's more structural theory of political change will be recognized now that translation has made his last monograph available to a wider audience. This final theory of politics posits a cycle between consolidation and erosion of central power. Movement on this cycle is characterized by changes in political structure, strategies of social control, and types and magnitude of opposition confronted by the regime in power. The striking difference between Pareto's final theory and his earlier version of "circulating elites" is that he abandons the implicit suggestion that an established elite is always going to be forcefully replaced. Political change does not have to be accompanied by revolution or substitution of regimes. Rather than focusing exclusively on changes in personnel, Pareto came to believe that we should employ a more structural analysis to the study of politics by focusing on organizational changes in the structure of political control.

FORCE VERSUS CO-OPTATION: STRATEGIES OF SOCIAL CONTROL

Pareto was fundamentally interested in the means different regimes use to establish and maintain order. This concern serves as a starting point because it is the foundation for his later theory of "consolidation and erosion of central authority" as well as his earlier theory of "circulation of elites."

Every regime bases its power on a combination of force and co-optation. Some regimes rely almost exclusively on one form of control whereas other regimes employ a mixed strategy for rule. Regimes employing a mixed strategy tend to be more stable than those that rely on only one tool (force or co-optation, but not both). So the character of government depends largely on the strategies employed for maintenance of social control.

> The inclination to rule through use of force and the inclination to rule by obtaining consensus often appear separately and in opposition. Exceptional individuals can have both sets of inclinations and accompanying skills, but the majority of governors tend to rely on the one much more than the other. The fundamental character of the society changes cyclically as classes circulate and as one inclination replaces another.[3]

The danger of relying on a single strategy for social control is most readily apparent in the case of authoritarian regimes. Although the use of force can be very effective in squashing dissent, it can also generate virulent hatred among ordinary citizens. A government that alienates its people runs the risk of spawning more resistance than it is capable of controlling. This was a lesson the Shah learned in Iran and the Samosa family learned in Nicaragua. It is one of the clearest lessons of history. A regime cannot long rule through the use of force alone. A stable regime must have a considerable degree of voluntary compliance, for the costs of effective surveillance and enforcement outweigh tax revenues when a population is recalcitrant.[4]

It is less obvious but just as surely true that no regime can enjoy any measure of long-term stability when it relies exclusively on co-optation as a means of social control. Many regimes try to ensure that they have support by co-opting powerful interest groups. Government subsidies, monopoly rights, lucrative contracts, and tariff barriers are frequently used to co-opt the support of industrialists. Certification procedures, board requirements, and fee setting have been used on occasion to placate powerful professional groups such as doctors, lawyers, and accountants. Minimum wage guarantees and closed-shop rules are used to satisfy labor unions. Social security benefits and public facilities are often provided in order to satisfy ordinary citizens. So the conclusion one must reach is that there are any number of policies and programs a regime can support in order to appeal to big voting blocs and powerful interests. Regimes that rule through co-optation can even try to placate opposing groups by advocating a variety of different kinds of programs for people with conflicting interests (e.g., a guaranteed price structure for farmers, which creates upward pressure on food prices, and a food stamp program, which reduces the cost of food for welfare recipients).

The great danger of democratic government is that regimes are tempted to placate many powerful interest groups in order to stay in power. It is for this reason that democracies can easily degenerate into demagogic plutocracies. They are demagogic when power ultimately rests on manipulation of ideology and rhetorical appeal to the masses. They are plutocratic when actual power resides in the hands of a small elite that rules through manipulation, placation, and coalition.

Speaking in a rather vague and loose way, the growing power of wealthy speculators might be viewed as a "plutocratic" tendency while the growing power of wage earners might be viewed as a "democratic" tendency.

Fourth, these two classes can be thought of as having in some sense cooperatively united or formed a partial alloy. This trend has been particularly apparent since the end of the nineteenth century. Even though the interests of speculators and workers do not correspond completely, it happens that certain members of both classes find it profitable to operate in the same way—to impose themselves upon the state and use it to exploit the remaining social classes. It also follows that plutocrats are able to force an effective union because they are astute and can deceive the masses by manipulating public sentiment. This gives rise to the widely observed phenomenon of demagogic plutocracy.[5]

Demagogic plutocracy eventually undermines prosperity and destroys government capacity to rule. For too much attention is paid to diverting wealth rather than creating it. To the misfortune of plutocratic regimes, the desires of those the regime tries to co-opt are insatiable. A group that is placated today will want more tomorrow, and this eventually bankrupts the system and leaves the regime unable to ensure continued support or compliance.

Pareto was convinced that overreliance on a single instrument of control (force or co-optation) generates problems for the regime in power, and these problems necessitate change. He initially posited that change takes form in the replacement of one regime by another, or by "circulation of elites." Although Pareto subsumed this analysis within a more sophisticated structural theory at the end of his life, he never altogether rejected his original imagery. It therefore merits attention, with the caveat that Pareto's final theory of politics is yet to follow.

PARETO'S EARLY THEORY OF POLITICS: THE CIRCULATION OF ELITES

Pareto defines elites as people who are either among the most outstanding practitioners or are among those wielding the greatest influence in their respective fields of endeavor.[6] The governing elite is a subset thereof. The governing elite is made up of those few people who make important government decisions and implement important government policies.

Inheritance of status is important, and those born with special advantages are more likely to enjoy influence than are persons born without advantages. Nonetheless, history demonstrates that there is, on the whole, a considerable amount of mobility in and out of the governing elite.[7] Mobility sometimes occurs because a regime recruits bright young people and sometimes because energetic people force their way into positions of authority. It is often difficult to remember, but elites really can be replaced.

> Where, in France, are the descendants of the Frankish conquerors? The genealogies of the English nobility have been very exactly kept; and they show that very few families still remain to claim descent from the comrades of William the Conqueror. The rest have vanished. In Germany the aristocracy of the present day is very largely made up of descendants of vassals of the lords of old.[8]

The old elite vanishes, although an illusion of continuity is often perpetuated by a new elite wishing to claim the legitimacy and authority that historical tradition seems to bestow.

> In virtue of class-circulation, the governing *elite* is always in a state of slow and continuous transformation. It flows on like a river, never being today what it was yesterday. From time to time sudden and violent disturbances occur. There is a flood—the river overflows its banks. Afterwards, the new governing *elite* again resumes its slow transformation. The flood has subsided, the river is again flowing normally in its wonted bed.[9]

Rapid changes not infrequently occur because an established elite has lost the will to use force, making it susceptible to overthrow.[10] Mobility, or circulation, produces change in the character of the elite. "Whether certain theorists like it or not, the fact is that human society is not a homogeneous thing, that individuals are physically, morally, and intellectually different."[11] When a regime either absorbs or is replaced by new people, the traits and inclinations predominant in the ruling class also change, ipso facto.

As would be expected, Pareto continues to focus on changes in the balance of sentiments. Persistence of aggregates, which remains relatively strong in the general population and often manifests itself in faith and religious commitment, tends to deteriorate in the governing elite. The "circulation of elites" often entails social movements driven by the revulsion that parochial and conservative masses feel for rulers who seem too decadent and greedy.[12] "The Protestant Reformation in the sixteenth century, the Puritan Revolution in Cromwell's day in England, the French Revolution of 1789, are examples of great religious tides originating in the lower classes and rising to engulf the skeptical higher classes."[13]

Pareto's analysis of the "circulation of elites" rests on the assumption that rulers who are strong in the sentiment of combinations are inclined (a) to be greedy and extract great sums of wealth from the nation in order to indulge their whims, and (b) to be weak and inept in the use of force. Hence, they become less capable of defending their privileges at the very time they most audaciously abuse those privileges. It is this combination of factors, both of which result from a disequilibrium or overabundance of sentiments of combination relative to sentiments of persistence of aggregates, that most endangers a regime.[14]

> When an elite declines, we can generally observe two signs which manifest themselves simultaneously: (1) The declining elite becomes softer, milder, more humane and less apt to defend its own power. (2) On the other hand, it does not lose its rapacity and greed for the goods of others, but rather tends as much as possible to increase its unlawful appropriations and to indulge in major usurpations of the national patrimony. Thus, on one hand it makes the yoke heavier, and on the other it has less strength to maintain it. These two conditions cause the catastrophe in which the elite perishes, whereas it could prosper if one of them were absent.[15]

One really cannot say whether the use of force is good or bad. Every combatant in a dispute uses force, physical or symbolic, to a greater or lesser degree. Most observers reach a judgment about whether the use of force was desirable or undesirable based on whether they approve of the winning side.[16] What we can say is that a government that loses the will or ability to employ force must rely on diplomacy for advancing its interests, and this is a very dangerous position in which to be. The Byzantine Empire was a major power for centuries, but crumbled at the heels of the Ottomans once its fate was entrusted to diplomacy. The Ottomans, in turn, forcefully extended their control from Algeria to the Persian Gulf and from Budapest to the Red Sea. But Turkey lost control of its vast foreign domains as soon as it lost its military advantage.[17]

The importance of force is a point Pareto emphasizes over and over again.[18]

> Advancing one step further, one notes that both in the fall of the Roman Republic and in the fall of the French monarchy, the respective governing classes were either unwilling or unable to use force, and were overthrown by other classes that were both willing and able to do that. Both in ancient Rome and in France the victorious element rose from the people and was made up in Rome of the legions of Sulla, Caesar, and Octavius, in France

of the revolutionary mobs that routed a very feeble royal power, and then of an army that vanquished the very inefficient troops of the European potentates.[19]

Lack of balance among sentiments destabilizes a regime. If too much reliance is placed on force as an instrument of social control, as is likely when the sentiment of group persistence dominates, common people are inclined to revolt under the weight of repression. When, on the other hand, the elite is dominated by people who are strong in Class I sentiments, control tends to be maintained through co-optation and chicanery.[20] Leaders conceal public debt, placate the powerful with concessions, and entice working people with grand shows, income maintenance programs, promises of public employment, and communal facilities.[21] Rule by co-optation can easily bankrupt a regime, promoting discontent and jealousy among people who are never satisfied with the advantages accruing to them because they feel deprived relative to others who enjoy more influence and therefore greater patronage.[22]

Unfortunately, elites have a habit of recruiting people like themselves. This tends to homogenize the ruling class and purge useful diversity of talent. It saps the strength of the elite.

> Governing classes that are rich in Class II residues but short in combination-instincts (Class I residues) need new elements in which those proportions are reversed. Such elements would ordinarily be supplied by normal circulation. But if, instead, the governing class opens its doors only to individuals who consent to be like it, and are indeed driven by their ardour as neophytes to exaggerate in that direction, the already harmful predominance of certain residues is carried further still and the road to ruin is thrown open. Conversely, a class, such as our plutocracy, that is woefully lacking in Class II residues and overrich in Class I residues would need to acquire new elements that are weak in Class I and strong in Class II residues.[23]

True circulation is quite desirable. It promotes prosperity and strengthens the society.[24] This is why history often records a spurt of prosperity following revolutions, because revolutions typically involve a sudden surge of new talent into a governing elite that had rigidified.[25]

Hence, the correction of some previous imbalance in sentiments is likely to result in temporary improvement in socioeconomic and political conditions. But what starts out as a desirable change has undesirable consequences if carried to any extreme. People then react in the opposite direction and a pendulous cycle is inaugurated. Consider the period following the accession of Augustus as Emperor of Rome. Force and courage replaced co-optation and cunning in government. Bribery and corruption declined somewhat, with a corresponding increase in general prosperity.

> But just as the old form of government produced a period of prosperity and then a period of decline, so the new form of government is to show a similar evolution; and just as the earlier period had revealed first the good points and then the bad points of government depending primarily on cunning (Class I residues), the new period is to show first the good points and then the bad points of a government resting primarily on force (Class II residues).[26]

One really cannot ask what form of government or economy is best: monarchy, republic, oligarchy, democracy, dictatorship, capitalist, socialist, feudal.[27] Politicians are the same all over the world and in every age. They propagate false information and manipulate the sentiments of the masses. They use whatever power is at their disposal (guns and patronage) in order to maximize personal interests.[28] A major problem presents itself when regimes become decadent. Their rule is then extravagant, wasteful, and characterized by graft and favoritism. Pareto tended to think of such elites as degenerate and unable to defend themselves against an overthrow by strong leaders emerging from the populace. If an overthrow does occur, the style of government changes with infusion of new people motivated by different sentiments. But over time, the new regime also tends to become decadent and the cycle begins anew.

This was Pareto's early theory of politics, the theory of "circulating elites." Near the end of his life, Pareto's thinking had developed and he advanced a more structural theory of political organization. It is Pareto's final and more sophisticated theory in which we are most interested and will explore in the next section.

CONSOLIDATION VERSUS EROSION OF AUTHORITY: PARETO'S LATER THEORY OF POLITICS

Pareto's portrayal of circulating elites has captured the imaginations of many people. This is unfortunate in a way, for Pareto came to regard his theory of circulating elites as embryonic and immature. Even in the face of widespread popular discontent, regimes are seldom forcefully overthrown. Cataclysmic change is far from an everyday event. On the contrary, political regimes and governmental institutions often enjoy great longevity. So if we really want to develop a theory of politics that has general use, we need to think about much more than the bloody overthrow of a few decadent rulers.

By the end of his career, Pareto advanced a theory of politics that was much more sophisticated and compelling than his theory of "circulation of elites." The new theory retains a common thread with the old, because Pareto continued to insist that force and co-optation are the main techniques that can be used to consolidate political power. But in his later writings, Pareto focused on types of political organization more than the personalities of leaders. Centralized power tends to rest on the use of force and a cult of personal control, whereas decentralized power tends to use co-optation and the delegation of authority. There is a tendency for organizational strategies to be modified whenever power and authority begin to erode.

In the most simple terms, power is greatest when a regime is adept at the use of both force and co-optation (carrot and stick) and is able to delegate working authority without parceling out its own sovereignty. However, failure to use both force and co-optation effectively results in an erosion of power. The more centralized political organization becomes, the more likely it is to turn into a cult of personal control resting exclusively on force to ensure compliance, and this produces organizational problems. Conversely, the more decentralized political organization becomes, the more likely the regime is to parcel out its own sovereignty and rely on co-optation to ensure compliance, which also produces problems of control. The greater the extent to which power erodes, the more pressure a regime will be under to modify its control strategies.

Many people have trouble with the concept of centralization. Any system of political or hierarchical organization can be either centrally or decentrally organized. "An organizational hierarchy is centralized if there are long chains of people who report one to another in one direction and who pass orders in the other; it is decentralized if people pass along few orders and reports along the chain and themselves initiate actions at many points."[29] Both centralized and decentralized systems can work well, but they can also be ineffective and weak. Pareto's final work, *The Transformation of Democracy*, is actually a case study the way power can erode when a state becomes too decentralized. Yet, it must be kept in mind that this book covers only one part of the cycle between centralization and decentralization through which Pareto thought all governments go.[30] Centralization has certain practical advantages but, if carried too far, leads to an erosion of political power that can only be reversed through decentralization. Decentralization has other practical advantages but, if carried too far, leads to an erosion of political power that can only be reversed through centralization.

As was so often the case, Pareto contributed to confusion by his use of terminology, and people who refer to Pareto's original works should keep certain terminological difficulties in mind. In the first place, Pareto frequently discusses "central government." The central government can be organized in either a centralized or a decentralized fashion. So "central government" merely refers to the main seat of power and not to the organizational strategy upon which government is based. For example, the United States has a federal system of government that is in many respects decentralized. This does not prevent us from referring to federal offices in Washington as the central government.

A second terminological problem is introduced with discussions of centripetal and centrifugal force. Pareto sometimes uses these terms as synonyms for centralization and decentralization of power. At other times, he uses centripetal and centrifugal force to refer to the consolidation and erosion of political power and authority.[31] Care must be taken because centralization and decentralization cannot be equated automatically with consolidation and erosion of power. Centralized governments can experience erosion of power just as decentralized governments can experience a consolidation of power. Either organizational design can be reasonably effective under certain circumstances.

If an erosion of power does occur, it by no means necessitates a drastic or revolutionary circulation of elites. A regime is always well advised to assimilate the most capable members of the non-elite population, thus making servants and pawns of those who pose the greatest potential threat. Revolutions only occur when a regime shows very little skill at using for its own purposes the leading elements of subordinate populations. So, in its most drastic form, where a decadent elite succumbs to a revolution arising from subordinate strata, the theory of circulating elites only applies to a few unusual cases. On the other hand, alternating periods of political centralization and decentralization are ubiquitous features of sociopolitical history.[32] Pareto's later theory is consequently more useful than his earlier theory.

The central point to remember is that Pareto really described a cycle between centralization and decentralization of power governed by trends toward consolidation or erosion of authority. Authority is relatively intact when a regime has the power (whether through centralized or decentralized apparatuses) and the will to adjudicate grievances and dispense justice throughout its realm. Authority erodes when governments lose the capacity for effective and independent action. This happens in some decentralized systems when concerted problem solving is precluded because the regime panders to special interests and parcels out its sovereignty to various power blocs. Erosion of power can also occur in centralized systems, as happens when embattled rulers asphyxiate the social structure by their failure to delegate meaningful authority to functionaries, or use force so capriciously that their rule is hated and their edicts obeyed only when soldiers are present to enforce them at the point of a gun.

> Central power is weakened during periods when centrifugal force gains momentum. It does not really matter whether the central power is monarchical, oligarchic, or popular in form. For "sovereignty" is a word that ceases to have much meaning as central power crumbles and covers the country with debris.[33]

History involves a continued repetition of this cycle between consolidation and erosion of authority.[34] To a certain extent, cyclical changes occur in patterns of political organization simply because of organizational constraints. Coordination and control become difficult in a bureaucracy that is thoroughly decentralized, just as they do in a governing apparatus that is thoroughly centralized. So we can speak of an elementary theory of political organization in the same way we spoke of elementary theories of popular sentiment and economic productivity. Organizational trends that gain momentum produce sources of strain and countervailing tendencies that result in an eventual reversal of the initial trends. The main elements of Pareto's elementary theory of political organization are propositionally stated in Table 9.1.[35]

Pareto's elementary theory of political organization suggests some of the dangers that can befall governing structures. There is an inherent tendency for decentralized governments to allow great autonomy to functionaries and special interests. But if this tendency proceeds too far it is equivalent to parceling out the authority to the state. For the state is

TABLE 9.1

An Elementary Theory of Political Organization

(1)	The greater the level of political decentralization (6), then (1) the more reliance there will be on co-optation as an instrument of social control and the greater the extent to which sovereignty will be parceled out to powerful interests.
(2)	The greater the extent of co-optation and parcelization of authority (1), then (2) the greater the danger that patronage and usufruct will undermine effective government.
(3)	The greater the level of organizational inefficiency resulting from ubiquitous patterns of patronage and usufruct (2), then (3) the more problematic coordination and control become and the more likely are reorganizational efforts aimed at centralization.
(4)	The greater the level of political centralization (3), then the greater the tendencies toward cult of personality and reliance on force as an instrument of control.
(5)	The less delegation of authority and the more punitive the system of social control (4), then (5) the fewer objectives the government apparatus will attempt to accomplish and the more likely it is to suffer from entropic asphyxiation.
(6)	The greater the level of organizational entropy resulting from failure to perform important functions, delegate authority, and to reward performance positively (5), then (6) the more problematic coordination and control become and the more likely are reorganizational efforts aimed at centralization.

impotent when powerful parties have too free a hand to promote their own interests. Centralized governments, on the other hand, tend to concentrate discretionary power and punish functionaries for independent initiative. This can be quite stifling. The greater the extent to which a few powerful individuals insist on controlling everything that happens, the less that gets done. This kind of government is little better than no government at all.

GENERAL SOCIOLOGY, PART II:
THE LINKAGE BETWEEN PUBLIC SENTIMENT
AND POLITICAL ORGANIZATION

The dynamics of ultimate interest to Pareto had to do with the linkage between public sentiment and political organization. Citizens are implicitly aware of the political strategies being used by a regime. Each strategy tends to promote certain values and retard others. Use of co-optation, for example, encourages people to view success in terms of who one knows rather than what one accomplishes. Widespread use of co-optation undermines the work ethic and stimulates hedonism. This change in public sentiment has, in turn, important consequences for government. A citizenry that has come to view the art of governing in

TABLE 9.2
General Sociology, Part II: Public Sentiment and Political Organization

(1)	The more fully centralized a regime is, the less responsive it is to the demands of diverse interests, and the more exclusively that it relies on force as an instrument of social control (6), then (1) the more widespread resistance will become, in part because people want governments to be active on their behalf and in part because the arbitrary use of force generates resentment.
(2)	The more widespread that resistance becomes (1), then (2) greater the erosion of government authority.
(3)	The greater the erosion of central authority in the face of resistance (2), then (3) the more likely a regime is to undergo decentralization, become more responsive to citizen demands, and rely more on co-optation as a control strategy, thus encouraging hedonistic attitudes and behavior.
(4)	The more fully decentralized a regime is, the more responsive it is to demands from diverse interests, the more exclusively that it relies on co-optation as an instrument of social control, and the more it encourages hedonism (3), then (4) the more patronage that people will expect and the greater the costs resulting from inefficiency, largess, and patronage.
(5)	The more patronage a regime grants and the more inefficient the system becomes (4), then (5) the greater the erosion of government authority.
(6)	The greater the erosion of government authority in the face of patronage and inefficiency (5), then (6) the more likely the regime is to centralize, become less responsive to citizens' demands, and rely on force as a control strategy.

terms of bribery, largess, and co-optation, wants to stand in line for its share of patronage, support, and benefits. A regime that relies upon co-optation will be confronted with a steady increase in demands for special treatment because human desires are insatiable and elastic, and because human values are retrogressive. That is, (1) the more people get, the more they think they deserve, and (2) people would rather get things the easy way than struggle by working for a living at an honest rate of remuneration. A government that dispenses patronage jobs, special licenses, monopoly rights, and other gratuities will soon find that everyone wants guarantees of special treatment. And this is simply more than most regimes can afford.[36] So by considering the linkages between public sentiment, economic productivity, and political organization, a much clearer picture of the dynamics of political organization can be arrived at.

Pareto's case study, *The Transformation of Democracy*, is illustrative. By 1920, Italy was, in Pareto's estimation, facing a crisis; the perceptible erosion of government authority. Union members openly flaunted their ability to defy the law and corporate giants were granted whatever concessions and supports they requested. The government seemed completely impotent in the face of organized interest groups. This raises what was, for Pareto, a crucial issue. If a regime is incapable of resisting the unreasonable demands of some, it is equally incapable of defending the rights of others. "The capacity of some people to avoid justice is a sure sign that central power is crumbling, just as the necessity of submitting to state jurisdiction is a sure sign of the ascendence of central power."[37]

These principles suggest a close interdependence between Pareto's elementary theory of social sentiment and his elementary theory of political organization.[38] The most important elements in the elementary theory of social sentiment, such as hedonism, influence and in turn are influenced by the most important elements in his elementary theory of political organization, such as patronage. As a result, changes in political organization have substantial impact on social sentiment, and vice versa. Developments in the political realm can impede or hasten trends in popular sentiment and trends in popular sentiment can foster or retard trends in the political arena. It is for precisely this reason that Pareto urged the development of "general sociology" as a unified science paying attention to the linkages among economics, politics, and social sentiment.

It is exceedingly important to consider the dynamics linking these cycles because we find that changes in political organization come about partially as a result of sociological dynamics and vice versa. The effectiveness of a given strategy for social control depends upon the climate of popular sentiment. When the sentiment of combinations prevails, people are self-interested and can think of little more than their own comfort. In such periods, it becomes futile to rely solely on co-optation as an instrument of control because people's desires for wealth and prestige are infinitely elastic.

The irony is that reliance on co-optation tends to encourage further this sentiment in the general public, and hence make governance more difficult. Patronage makes people ask when their piece of the pie will arrive. This is not true only of the middle class. Members of less-advantaged groups come to believe that they have never been and never will be included equitably in the distribution of resources. And at the same time that they come to believe they have been "left out," they begin to feel a sense of revulsion from what they regard as the greed and decadence of all privileged groups, and they begin to demand more benefits for themselves.

Overreliance on force has the opposite effect. When common people come to feel that enforcement of the law is blind, capricious, and rigid, it creates a widespread sense of resistance.

TABLE 9.3
General Sociology, Part III:
Economic Productivity and Political Organization

(1) The harder it is to transact business (6), then (1) the more pressure there will be for government restructuring.
(2) The more decentralized political organization becomes (1), then (2) the more extensive the use of co-optation, and hence, the greater the number of and more diverse the array of special interests that are granted protection and operational freedom.
(3) The more widespread co-optation becomes (2), then (3) the greater encouragement there is for production of inferior products for sale at high prices.
(4) The lower the ratio between product quality and cost (3), then (4) the more pressure there will be for government restructuring.
(5) The more centralized political organization becomes (4), then (5) the less well developed and coordinated societal infrastructure will be.
(6) The more infrastructural problems there are (5), then (6) the harder it is to transact business.

GENERAL SOCIOLOGY, PART III: ECONOMICS AND POLITICAL ORGANIZATION

Linkages between the economy and political organization are the least developed aspects of Pareto's general sociology.[39] He actually had very little to say beyond free-market polemics, thus forcing us to move cautiously into the domain of speculation. What does seem clear is that Pareto recognized the deadening effect an overbearing bureaucracy can have on business.[40] Pareto's general train of thought can be succinctly stated in a series of propositions emphasizing the ways that trends in political organization can influence the national economy.

Once again, the implication is clear. Business conditions are affected by the nature of political organization as well as purely technical factors involving land, materials, labor, and equipment. By the same token, economic trends exert predictable patterns of influence on the polity. Interdependence between the economy and polity must be taken into consideration by anyone hoping to understand society well enough to make predictions about future developments.[41]

In its most simple formulation, Pareto's theory suggests that governments undergo long-term structural reorganization regardless of whether leadership changes or not. Thus, his final theory of politics is more generalizable than his earlier allusions to a revolutionary "circulation of elites." Highly centralized governments come under pressure to change because they are not responsive enough to really serve the public interest. But highly decentralized governments come under pressure for exactly the opposite reason. They are too responsive to too many interests. A government that is unwilling to prevent unreasonable actions or deny unreasonable demands made by some interest groups is equally incapable of protecting the real interests of average citizens. Such governments lose effective control, spawning great injustice and inefficiency, by parceling out carte blanche operating autonomy to power blocs, vested interests, petty functionaries, and subordinate organizational units. This is why the American political system had to undergo some centralization in the 1960s, with the federal government assuming a greater range of functions. This was an effort to stem abuse of civil liberties committed in the name of states' rights and an attempt to contain evironment pollution generated in the name of corporate freedom.[42]

By presenting separate bodies of elementary theory covering social sentiment, economic productivity, and political organization, and then by examining the nature of mutual dependency among sentiments, productivity, and political structure, Pareto provides us with a holistic framework for understanding society and predicting change. These are the ingredients of his "general sociology."[43]

NOTES

1. Vilfredo Pareto, *The Rise and Fall of the Elites*, introduced by Hans Zetterberg (Totowa, NJ: Bedminster, 1968); originally published in 1901.

2. Vilfredo Pareto, *The Transformation of Democracy*, ed. Charles Powers (R. Girola, trans.) (New Brunswick, NJ: Transaction Books, 1984); originally published in 1921. This revised theory is examined by Powers in "Vilfredo Pareto's Real Theory of Politics."

3. Ibid., p. 57.

4. Ray Maghroori and S. Gorman, "The Conceptual Weakness of American Foreign Policies Toward Authoritarian Third World Allies," *Townson State Journal of International Relations* 16, 2 (1980, Spring): 57-73.

5. Pareto, *Transformation,* p. 55.

6. Vilfredo Pareto, *The Mind and Society* (hereafter, *Treatise* Section 2031-2033, ed. Arthur Livingston (A. Bongiorno and A. Livingston with J. H. Rogers, trans.) (New York: Harcourt Brace Jovanovich, 1935); reprinted by Dover in 1963 and AMS in 1983 under the original 1916 title, *Treatise on General Sociology.*

7. Ibid., sections 2025, 2036.

8. Ibid., section 2053.

9. Ibid., section 2056.

10. Ibid., section 2057.

11. Ibid., section 2025.

13. Ibid., section 2050.

14. Pareto, *Elites*, p. 68.

15. Ibid., p. 59.

16. Pareto, *Treatise*, sections 2174-2175.

17. Ibid., section 2180.

18. Ibid., section 2191.

19. Ibid., section 2199.

20. Ibid., section 2228.

21. Ibid., section 2255.

22. Pareto, *Transformation*.

23. Pareto, *Treatise*, section 2484.

24. Ibid., section 2485.

25. Ibid., seciton 2487.

26. Ibid., section 2549.

27. Ibid., section 2239.

28. Ibid., section 2267.

29. Randall Collins, with a contribution by J. Annett, *Conflict Sociology* (New York: Academic Press, 1975), p. 316.

30. Pareto, *Transformation*, chapter 3.

31. Ibid., p. 37.

32. Ibid., chapter 5.

33. Ibid., p. 41.

34. Ibid., p. 37.

35. These principles are an amended version of past efforts. See Charles Powers, "Pareto's Theory of Society," *Revue européenne des sciences sociales et cahiers Vilfredo Pareto*, 19, 59 (1981): 99-119.

36. Pareto, *Transformation*, chapter 3.

37. Ibid., pp. 45-46.

38. Charles Powers and Robert Hanneman, "Pareto's Theory of Social and Economic Cycles: A Formal Model and Simulation," *Sociological Theory* 1 (1983): 59-89.

39. Charles Powers, "Sociopolitical Determinants of Economic Cycles," *Social Science Quarterly* 65, 4 (1984, December): 988-1001.

40. Vilfredo Pareto, *La Liberté économique et les événements d'Italie* (New York: Burt Franklin, 1968).

41. Pareto, *Transformation*.

42. Ibid.

43. Powers and Hanneman, *Social and Economic Cycles*.

10

Conclusion
Pareto's "General Sociology" Reconsidered

Pareto's stated objective was to derive inductively social scientific principles from field observations and historical research, and then to link these into an integrated, deductive theory of society. Unfortunately, Pareto fell short of accomplishing his mission. Certain that he intuitively understood the operating dynamics of social systems, he was nevertheless unable to translate his rambling thoughts and discursive treatises into the kind of succinct and testable theoretical propositions that are required for deductive theory. Pareto understood that he had not gone the last mile when he wrote,

> at this stage a deductive track would be artificial. It would be wiser to employ that approach at a later date after further studies have strengthened the foundations of the theory. In the meantime it is useful to continue following the inductive approach attempting to confirm our initial conclusions.[1]

Although Pareto was unable to complete the task he set for himself, he came very close. His empirical generalizations describe societal dynamics in their rough contours, and these generalizations clearly suggest a set of theorems as outlined in Chapters 7-9. We can precisely specify these theorems, even if Pareto was unable to verbalize them in his own lifetime. By doing so we put ourselves well on the way toward accomplishing the theoretical goal Pareto set for himself: developing a science of society.[2] It seems clear that Pareto would have wanted us to exercise this license and formalize his ideas into a set of principles.

> If, accordingly, one would remould the social sciences on the model of the natural sciences, one must proceed in them as the natural sciences, reducing highly complicated concrete phenomena to simpler theoretical phenomena, being exclusively guided all the while by the intent to discover experimental uniformities, and judging the efficacy of what one has done only by the experimental verifications that may be made of it.[3]

This concluding chapter is an attempt to fulfill Pareto's mission. His general sociology will be outlined in clear terms and specified by the theoretical principles presented in earlier chapters. There can be no doubt that Pareto was one of the great masters of sociological theory. His insights were quite penetrating and continue to be valuable for all that they reveal.

THE SOCIAL SYSTEM

Pareto's general sociology is predicated on the assumption that societies are really *systems* of social relations. This assumption has far-reaching implications. Systems are composed of interdependent elements, so any event affecting part of the system can have consequences for the whole.

The recognition that societies are social systems carried a very practical implication for Pareto as an economist. Economic trends can only be adequately understood if proper attention is paid to sociopolitical as well as economic aspects of the social system. This conclusion launched Pareto on his search for a "general sociology," or a science of social systems, to integrate the studies of popular sentiment, political organization, and economic productivity.

SOCIAL CYCLES

One implication of the concept of social system is that anything can have an effect on anything else. This makes standard causal modeling seem not only futile, but also rather infantile. So Pareto forsook the traditional social science method of selecting a single event to be explained by tracing the immediate antecedents of that event. Instead, he tried to clear his mind of preconceptions and ask what generalizations one might reach about long-term patterns of societal change. In his estimation, the most striking lesson offered by history is that events oscillate. Good times precede and follow bad, and bad times precede and follow good. Cyclical dynamics must be at work, and this is where Pareto began his search.

A dedicated empiricist, Pareto's first step was to embark on a program of careful observation. And what he observed was rather startling. The good times and bad that societies move through are actually three separate but synchronized cycles: cycles in social sentiment, economic productivity, and political organization. Periods of social constraint precede and follow periods of relative freedom. Periods of economic prosperity precede and follow times of scarcity and stagnation. And periods of political centralization precede and follow periods of decentralization.

Pareto observed that all three cycles tend to oscillate at approximately the same time, although the cycle of popular sentiment may tend to lag somewhat behind the other cycles. This suggests that the cycles are synchronized in some way. That is, they are somehow related and tend to spur each other. The character of a society at any given historical period reflects its position on these synchronized cycles. Economies expand, politics decentralize, and social constraint is relaxed, all at about the same time. Economic contraction, political centralization, and increased social constraint also seem to occur coterminously, although changes in social sentiment tend to lag somewhat behind the other two cycles.[4]

This put Pareto well on his way in the process of developing his theory of "general sociology." Sentiments, productivity, and political organization all undergo undulatory change. So three separate sets of cyclical dynamics must be at work. In addition, each cycle is linked with the others, and the nature of this synchronized interdependence needed to be defined. Thus, Pareto's general sociology took form as he attempted to define six separate sets of operating dynamics: dynamics intrinsic to each of the three cycles and the dynamics linking each pair of cycles. Until that time, Pareto's sociological investigations had been essentially empirical. He tried to record events and observe regularities. It was at this point that the difficult theoretical work began.

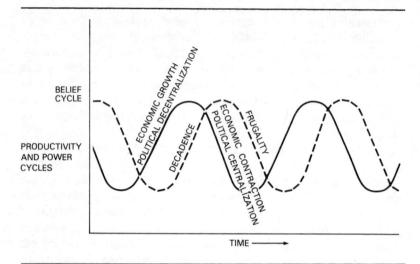

Figure 10.1   The General Form of Society

Pareto had to discover what cyclical dynamics are at work in social systems. Trends in one direction generate forces of resistance that eventually halt and then reverse the direction of change. Change in that new direction proceeds slowly at first and then gains momentum. But at the very time that change in a given direction is gaining momentum, forces of resistance also accumulate. As resistance builds, the forward momentum of change is slowed. Change grinds to a halt and is then reversed, producing another pendulous cycle.[5] The economy, politics, and public sentiment each display cyclical change over time, and each cycle acts to synchronize the others. That is why societal change produces rhythmic patterns in history.[6]

AN ELEMENTARY THEORY OF SOCIAL SENTIMENT

The cycle of sentiment is dealt with at length in Chapter 7. There are periods when the people in a society come to feel, on aggregate, as though behavioral proscriptions are too rigid, overly constraining, and too arbitrary in their application. When this mood grips a populace, people begin questioning the wisdom of traditional beliefs, and they come to feel that there are many circumstances under which even good rules should be waived.

This mood makes people receptive to new ideas and legitimates deviation from conventional behavior. The prevailing sentiment enables people to challenge traditional proscriptions and also encourages toleration. Furthermore, it fosters a certain degree of hedonism and self-centered evaluation of what is good.

This shift in mood has many consequences. The most striking is that it enables people, indeed even encourages them, to challenge constantly the boundaries of permissibility. Social conventions are relaxed. People come to feel more free and less constrained. It is important to remember that this new-found freedom will be truly welcome by a population reacting against an old system of rigid, arbitrary, outmoded rules. And the more welcome the new freedom is, the more justified people feel in further challenging social conventions.

Herein lies a dilemma. Many social proscriptions are quite useful. Among other things they help protect us against harm inflicted by others. For example, a dormitory resident who plays a loud stereo disturbs, without necessarily intending to, other students who may wish to rest, study, or contemplate events of the day. The simple fact is that as social proscriptions are dropped, people are more likely to harm others unwittingly. And the more often the average citizen is harmed, inconvenienced, or offended by others, the more likely citizens are to reach a consensus that freedom has gone too far and more constraint would be desirable. This new social climate legitimates the application of old conventions and fosters the proliferation of new ones. Hazy college classrooms were filled with plumes of cigarette smoke in the freedom-loving 1960s. It was in the conservative 1970s that students admonished professors and classmates to extinguish their smokes.

If people reach the conclusion that a society *should* be more orderly, they tend to like the initial consequences of any trend toward greater social constraint. This legitimates still further efforts to generate and enforce rigid rules. But, as noted earlier, the proliferation and enforcement of rules can only go so far before a reaction sets in and people long for greater freedom. These are the cyclical dynamics that produce undulatory change in sentiment. People long for definitive rules that provide clear guidelines for behavior and they long for the freedom to abrogate the rules they find inconvenient. But we cannot really have it both ways.

This dilemma fuels undulatory change. Greater freedom is encouraged when the collective feeling seems to be that rules are too restrictive. Movement to relax social conventions gains momentum as long as there is an underlying consensus that existing norms are too constraining. But the more relaxed conventions become, the less protection they provide and the less definitive they are as guides for behavior. Once people become disillusioned, a reaction starts in the opposite direction.

AN ELEMENTARY THEORY OF SOCIAL SENTIMENT

(1) The more equivocal norms become (6), then (1) the less constrained people are in their behavior and the more likely actions of potential but unproven detriment to others are to be tolerated.

(2) The less constraining norms are, and the more tolerant people are of actions of potential but unproven detriment (1), then (2) the more confusion there is likely to be over definitions of appropriate behavior and the more likely people are to be injured or offended by the imprudent actions of others.

(3) The more confusion there is over definitions of appropriate behavior and the more injury and offense people sustain due to the imprudent actions of others (2), then (3) the more likely people are to seek coherent traditions and unequivocal proscriptions.

(4) The less equivocal proscriptions become (3), then (4) the more constrained people and the more likely people are to fear being blamed for the anticipated and unanticipated consequences of their actions.

(5) The more constraining norms are and the more inhibited people are out of fear of blame (4), then (5) the more likely people are to question the rationality of normative beliefs and the more likely people are to avoid helping others.

(6) The more people question the rationality of beliefs and the more hesitant people are to cooperate with others (5), then (6) the more likely they are to seek relaxed proscriptions and freedom of autonomous action.

AN ELEMENTARY THEORY OF ECONOMIC PRODUCTIVITY

Economic cycles are dealt with at length in Chapter 8. According to Pareto, the purely economic forces at work producing cyclical change revolve around capital investment. Investment of capital in new enterprises generates economic growth. And with prosperity comes certain structural changes, including the increasing importance of consumer-oriented sectors that tend to have relatively high rates of depreciation. This means that the need for replacement capital increases steadily because prosperous economies have big infrastructures with high rates of depreciation. So the bigger an economy is, the more replacement capital is needed, even to maintain a no-growth situation. Yet, the need for replacement capital is greatest at the very time that the capacity of the economy to produce investment capital is undermined by the growing importance of consumer sectors relative to capital-producing sectors. Economic downturn sets in at such time that need exceeds the availability of replacement capital.

When investment falls short of depreciation, the economy contracts and prosperity declines. Consumption diminishes, businesses fail, and the economic infrastructure withers. The consumer sector is particularly hard hit during most recessions. And aggregate investment tends to decline because of the prevailing climate of uncertainty. But the need for replacement capital diminishes because a shrunken infrastructure characterized by a low rate of depreciation has less to maintain. Moreover, the capital-producing sectors grow relative to consumer-oriented sectors. A reservoir of capital accumulates, business climate improves, investment increases, growth is stimulated, and the cycle renews itself.

Propositions:

(1) The greater the availability of capital and will to invest (6), then (1) the more probable that economic expansion becomes.

(2) The greater the increase in productivity (1), then (2) the greater the expansion of consumer-oriented sectors of the economy relative to capital-producing sectors.

(3) The larger the economy (1) and the lower the relative commitment of resources to production of capital (2), then (3) the greater the replacement needs resulting from depreciation, the greater the probability of capital shortages, and the more hesitant people will be (as a result of high interest rates) to invest in the expansion of industry.

(4) The more serious capital shortages become and the more hesitant people are to invest in expansion of basic industries (3), then (4) the more probable economic contraction becomes.

(5) The more productivity declines (4), then (5) the greater the decline of consumer-oriented sectors relative to capital-producing sectors of the economy.

(6) The smaller the economy and the greater the relative commitment of resources to the production of capital (5), then (6) the lower the

replacement needs resulting from depreciation, the greater the availability of capital, and the less hesitant people will be to invest in economic
expansion.

GENERAL SOCIOLOGY, PART I:
SOCIAL SENTIMENT AND ECONOMIC PRODUCTIVITY

Pareto was not particularly satisfied with his elementary theories of
social sentiment and economic productivity. That is precisely the reason
he sought to advance a theory of "general sociology." Social or
economic or political theories in isolation are bound to be inadequate.
The most interesting and important societal dynamics are not social or
economic or political. Rather, they involve the interfacing dynamics
that link changes in sentiment with economic productivity, changes in
sentiment with political organization, and changes in economic productivity with political organization.

To understand the nature of economic cycles truly, one must focus on
cycles in social sentiment. The opposite is also true. To understand the
cycles in sentiment one must be aware of changes in the economy. An
economy has its strongest foundation when citizens are hard working
and willing to delay gratification. But the most prosperous economy is
not always the one with the strongest foundation. Dramatic spurts in
economic growth tend to occur during periods of self-centered consumer hedonism. That is, economies are propelled to new heights by
people pampering themselves with cars, refrigerators, and stereos.
Expenditures for consumer durables generate business for the basic
industries that are the backbone of an industrial economy: steel,
electronics, petrochemicals, and so on. And make no mistake, there
must be some degree of self-centered hedonism to stimulate such
purchases. People have to be willing to part with hard-earned dollars for
the sake of short-term comfort. This is a reflection of sentiments, which
are sociological rather than economic phenomena. However, the more
prosperous an economy becomes, the more hedonistic citizens are
inclined to be. So there is clearly an element of mutual determination
linking social sentiment and economic productivity.

If hedonism promotes short-term growth, it just as surely undermines
long-term fortunes. For the greater the extent to which people indulge
their tastes for immediate gratification, the more they squander savings
and incur debt. In the long run, people are forced to curtail extravagant

living and use earnings to retire debts rather than acquire material possessions or indulge the whim for new thrills. Consumption declines, basic industries suffer, and the effects reverberate throughout the economy. These experiences make people more cautious and frugal. Hedonism recedes. Thus, it is only by being a sociologist that one can understand economic cycles, and it is only by being an economist that one can understand cycles in social sentiment.

Propositions:

(1) The greater the rate of increase in productivity (6), then (1) the more likely it is that increasing complexity and opportunity in life will bring traditional beliefs into conflict with actual experiences, with the result that there will be increased pressure for relaxation of social proscriptions.

(2) The more relaxed social proscriptions become (1), then (2) the more legitimate self-gratification becomes, thus encouraging a consumer-based economic boom and infrastructural transformation to a consumer-oriented economy.

(3) The greater the levels of consumer debt and infrastructural transformation to a consumer-oriented economy (2), then (3) the more scarce unutilized capital becomes and the more likely the economy is to contract.

(4) The greater the level of economic contraction (3), then (4) the greater the shortfall between aspirations and socioeconomic attainment, and the more restrictive social proscriptions are likely to become.

(5) The more constraining social proscriptions are (4), then (5) the less legitimate it will be to pursue self-gratification so that consumer spending diminishes, consumer-oriented industries are undermined, and the aggregate level of savings begins to increase.

(6) The greater the level of infrastructural transformation to a capital-producing economy and the greater the accumulation of private saving (5), then (6) the greater the reservoir of excess capital available for investment and the more likely a business-led economic recovery becomes.

AN ELEMENTARY THEORY OF POLITICAL ORGANIZATION

Pareto's elementary theory of political organization is advanced in Chapter 9. Some governments are decentralized. Authority is delegated to semi-autonomous functionaries enabling them to act effectively and to respond quickly in a changing environment. So decentralized governments can work quite well. However, there are potential problems. If functionaries have too much autonomy and are unaccountable, the government apparatus can become an inefficient tangle. In a government where functionaries are not accountable, subordinates can act with impunity. This emasculates rulers by enfeebling the machinery of government. It poses an implicit threat and generates pressure for centralization. Moreover, decentralized governments tend to allow freedom of action to powerful interest groups, engendering abuse and further pressure for centralization of power.

Centralization involves the concentration of decision-making authority in the hands of a few units or individuals. A central government reduces one set of problems by depriving functionaries of operating autonomy and by limiting its responsiveness to vested interests. But it simultaneously creates another set of problems, because very little can be accomplished by a government that is unresponsive and whose functionaries are afraid to exercise independent initiative. A government that does nothing triggers organizational pressures for restructuring.

Propositions:

(1) The greater the level of political decentralization (6), then (1) the more reliance there will be on co-optation as an instrument of social control and the greater the extent to which sovereignty will be parceled out to powerful interests.

(2) The greater the extent of co-optation and parcelization of authority (1), then (2) the greater the danger that patronage and usufruct will undermine effective government.

(3) The greater the level of organizational inefficiency resulting from ubiquitous patterns of patronage and usufruct (2), then (3) the more problematic coordination and control become and the more likely are reorganizational efforts aimed at centralization.

(4) The greater the level of political centralization (3), then (4) the greater the tendencies toward cult of personality and reliance on force as an instrument of control.

(5) The less delegation of authority and the more punitive the system of social control (4), then (5) the fewer objectives the government apparatus will attempt to accomplish and the more likely it is to suffer from entropic asphyxiation.

(6) The greater the level of organizational entropy resulting from failure to delegate authority and to reward performance positively (5), then (6) the

more problematic coordination and control become and the more likely are reorganizational efforts aimed at centralization.

GENERAL SOCIOLOGY, PART II: SOCIAL SENTIMENT AND POLITICAL ORGANIZATION

Pareto's elementary theory of politics, like his elementary theory of economy, is most interesting when considered with reference to changes in social sentiment. Decentralized governments encourage patronage, largess, and co-optation. They are susceptible to pressure from vested interests, and the work ethic is significantly undermined when people come to believe that rewards are determined by who one is irrespective of what one does. All these factors encourage people to make demands on the political system and to look to government as a dispenser of jobs and benefits. Unfortunately, there is a limit to the needs a government can assuage and the benefits it can bestow. This is especially true in countries where government employment is viewed as patronage, and where government functionaries consequently feel no need to be efficient or effective in the performance of their duties. The outcome must inevitably be the failure of the government to meet the rising expectations of citizens for free benefits and of powerful interests for special largess. The more pronounced these conditions become, the more pressure mounts for centralization.

Centralization reduces many of the inefficiencies associated with patronage, but it also tends to reduce sensitivity to input from citizens. Combined with the flagrant use of force common in some centralized systems, great resentment can well up against the established order. The more extreme popular resistance becomes, the more pressure mounts for political reorganization.

Propositions:

(1) The more fully centralized a regime is, the less responsive it is to the demands of diverse interests, and the more exclusively that it relies on force as an instrument of social control (6), then (1) the more widespread resistance will become, in part because people want governments to be active on their behalf and in part because the arbitrary use of force generates resentment.

(2) The more widespread that resistance becomes (1), then (2) the greater the erosion of government authority.

(3) The greater the erosion of central authority in the face of resistance (2), then (3) the more likely a regime is to undergo decentralization, become more responsive to citizen demands, and rely more on co-optation as a control strategy, thus encouraging hedonistic attitudes and behavior.

(4) The more fully decentralized a regime is, the more responsive it is to demands from diverse interests, the more exclusively that it relies on co-optation as an instrument of social control, and the more it encourages hedonism (3), then (4) the more patronage that people will expect and the greater the costs resulting from inefficiency, largess, and patronage.

(5) The more patronage a regime grants and the more inefficient the system becomes (4), then (5) the greater the erosion of government authority.

(6) The greater the erosion of government authority in the face of patronage and inefficiency (5), then (6) the more likely the regime is to centralize, become less responsive to citizens' demands, and rely on force as a control strategy.

GENERAL SOCIOLOGY, PART III: ECONOMIC PRODUCTIVITY AND POLITICAL ORGANIZATION

Pareto said much less than he might have been expected to say about the connection between economic and political cycles. But his message is plainly clear.[7] Some decentralized governments are efficient and can stimulate economic growth by providing planning and public infrastructure. But decentralized governments often evolve into unwieldy bureaucracies that impede rather than enhance the conduct of business. Economic growth is stifled to the degree that this occurs, and pressures mount for centralization. However, centralized administrations have their own characteristic shortcomings. In particular, centralized governments tend to be unresponsive to the needs of citizens. They can also be capricious in the exercise of force. Pressure for decentralization mounts as these qualities make themselves apparent.

Propositions:

(1) The harder it is to transact business (6), then (1) the more pressure there will be for government restructuring.

(2) The more decentralized political organization becomes (1), then (2) the more extensive the use of co-optation, and hence, the greater the number of and more diverse the array of special interests that are granted protection and operational freedom.

(3) The more widespread co-optation becomes (2), then (3) the greater encouragement there is for production of inferior products for sale at high prices.

(4) The lower the ratio between product quality and cost (3), then (4) the more pressure there will be for government restructuring.

(5) The more centralized political organization becomes (4), then (5) the less well developed and coordinated societal infrastructure will be.

(6) The more infrastructural problems there are (5), then (6) the harder it is to transact business.

THE GENERAL FORM OF SOCIETY

It is by focusing on the dynamics of mutual dependence among social sentiment, economic productivity, and political organization that Pareto constructs the same kind of equilibrium theory for society that he had worked with decades earlier as an engineering student investigating the dynamics of expansion and contraction in solids. When trends in one direction gain momentum, they can result in change in the opposite direction. Cyclical oscillation results. Cycles emerge in large part because social, economic, and political factors are interdependent. A trend on one cycle produces transformations on the second and third cycle, the reverberations of which first stimulate and then counteract the original trends. Thus, increased prosperity encourages hedonism, which stimulates consumer spending and economic growth in the short run but results in an accumulation of debt that can eventually ruin an economy. "If an existing state of social equilibrium is altered, forces tending to reestablish it come into play—that, no more, no less, is what equilibrium means. Such forces are, in chief, sentiments that find their expression in residues of the variety we are here examining."[8] Change is inevitable because every state generates forces of resistance that make static conditions untenable.

Change in social sentiment, economic prosperity, and political centralization occur coterminously, for the cycles in social sentiment, economic productivity, and political organization are synchronized. The "general form of society" changes as this undulatory pattern unfolds,[9] and the theoretical principles presented in this monograph are

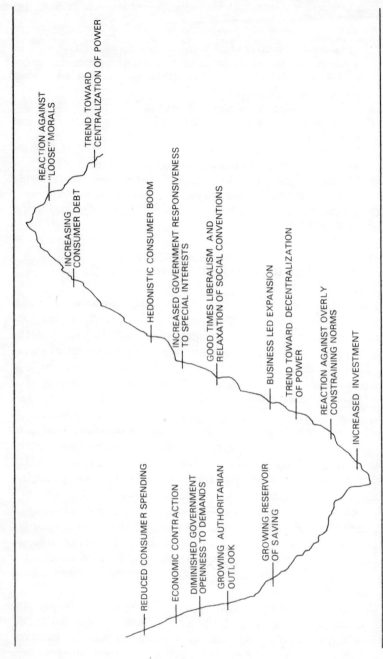

Figure 10.2 Pareto's General Sociology: Mutual Interdependence of Economy, Political Organization, and Social Sentiment

intended to help us model how and why those transformations take place.[10]

FINAL COMMENTS

The "general sociology" of Vilfredo Pareto is not without its problems. Pareto derived his theoretical generalizations by examining specific cases, notably ancient Greece and Rome, feudal Europe, and nineteenth-century Italy and France. He tended to assume that what was true for those places and times was generally true of all societies at all times. This was a dangerous assumption for Pareto to make. And there are more concrete problems. First, the elementary theory of sentiment presumes that most people find it easy, under a given set of conditions, to question the rigidity of social proscriptions or ethical texts. But the will to do this may vary markedly from culture to culture. For example, a people whose moral code derives from interpretation of parables (e.g., Christians) may find it easier to question than do people who believe their sacred texts to be the literal word of God and therefore infallible (e.g., Muslims). It is not clear that "liberalization" means the same thing, on a phenomenological level, in these two types of societies. Second, the tendency for capital to evaporate during expansionary periods is not as clear or pervasive as Pareto seems to imply, in part because Pareto's assumptions about shifting patterns of entrepreneurial activity and depreciation rates are rather faulty. Third, Pareto's model of the centralization and decentralization process also seems somewhat flawed. And we must be firm on this point. There most certainly are societies where the authority to make decisions is highly concentrated, but where patronage and co-optation is also widespread. Such societies seem to combine the worst characteristics of both forms of government. The capacity of government agencies to act in the best interest of the people is severely limited when functionaries have no discretionary power and are punished for showing initiative. At the same time, the capacity of government agencies to strangulate a society by impeding private initiative is greatest where there are large numbers of functionaries who are protected by patronage and who have no useful jobs and therefore nothing to do but scrutinize and delay the activities of private citizens who should be allowed to go about their business. Injection of the worst elements of both organizational strategies into the bureaucratic apparatus accounts for a portion of the morass that many nations find themselves in today.

But if Pareto's work has some weaknesses, it has many more strengths and isolates dynamics of fundamental and far-reaching importance that other social scientists have tended to ignore. Shifts in popular mood are inexorable because change in one direction (either more social constraint or more freedom) is always taken to extremes by people caught up in the prevailing sentiments of the times. Second, the rate and nature of economic expansion are largely determined by aggregate patterns of consumer saving and consumption, which are reflections of sentiment and inherently sociological rather than economic. The "roaring" 1920s and the unforgettable bust of the 1930s provide ample evidence of this point. And third, on those occasions when shifts in popular mood turn into a swell directed against the government, regimes collapse. Iran is a contemporary case. Among other things, this demonstrates the continuing power of religious conviction in much of the world, a power that should not be ignored by people attempting to construct theories of society. Pareto's theory is powerful and illuminating. The longer one's temporal horizons and the wider one's knowledge of the world, the more clear it becomes that Vilfredo Pareto was able to see beyond ephemeral events and actually identify major dynamics giving rise to social change.

NOTES

1. Vilfredo Pareto, *The Transformation of Democracy*, ed. Charles Powers (R. Girola, trans.) (New Brunswick, NJ: Transaction Books, 1984); originally published in 1921; p. 71, footnote 3.

2. Vilfredo Pareto, *The Mind and Society* (hereafter, *Treatise*), ed. Arthur Livingston (A. Bongiorno and A. Livingston with J. H. Rogers, trans.) (New York: Harcourt Brace Jovanovich, 1935); reprinted by Dover in 1963 and AMS in 1983 under the original 1916 title, *Treatise on General Sociology*.

3. Ibid., section 2411.

4. Charles Powers, "The Life and Times of Vilfredo Pareto," in Vilfredo Pareto, *The Transformation of Democracy*, ed. Charles Powers (R. Girola, trans.) (New Brunswick, NJ: Transaction Books, 1984); originally published in 1921.

5. Pareto, *Treatise*, section 2541.

6. Ibid., section 2552.

7. Pareto, *Transformation*.

8. Pareto, *Treatise*, section 1210.

9. Ibid., volume IV.

10. For a mathematical model see Charles Powers and Robert Hanneman, "Pareto's Theory of Social and Economic Cycles: A Formal Model and Simulation," *Sociological Theory* 1 (1983): 59-89.

Selected Bibliography

Some Central Works in Vilfredo Pareto's Sociology

1869
"Principi fondamentali della teoria della elasticité de' corpi solidi e ricerche sulla integrazione delle equazioni differenziali che ne definiscono l'equilibrio." Reprinted in Vilfredo Pareto, *Scritti teorici* (Milan: Malfasi, 1952, pp. 593-639).
1893
"The Parliamentary Regime in Italy." *Political Science Quarterly*, 1893, pp. 677-721. Reprinted in Vilfredo Pareto, *The Ruling Class in Italy Before 1900*, (New York: S.F. Vanni, 1950).
1896-1897
Cours d'économie politique (Geneva: Librairie Droz, 1964).
1898
La Liberté economique et les événements d'Italie (New York: Burt Franklin, 1968).
1901
The Rise and Fall of the Elites (Totowa, NJ: Bedminster Press, 1968). Introduced by Hans Zetterberg.
1902-1903
Les Systèmes socialistes (Geneva: Librairie Droz, 1965).
1909
Manual of Political Economy (2nd edition), eds. Ann Schwier and Alfred Page (A. Schwier, trans.) (New York: August M. Kelley, 1971).
1911
Le Mythe Vertuiste et la Littérature Immorale (Geneva: Librairie Droz, 1971).
1916
The Mind and Society, ed. Arthur Livingston (A. Bongiorno and A. Livingston with J. H. Rogers, trans.) (New York: Harcourt Brace Jovanovich, 1935); reprinted by Dover in 1963 and by AMS in 1983 under the original 1916 title, *Treatise on General Sociology*.
1920
Faits et Theories (Geneva: Librairie Droz, 1976).

1921

The Transformation of Democracy, ed. Charles Powers (R. Girola, trans.) (New Brunswick, NJ: Transaction Books, 1984).

Correspondence

Lettres 1860-1890, ed. Giovanni Busino (Geneva: Librairie Droz, 1981.

Correspondance 1890-1923, ed. Giovanni Busino (Geneva: Librairie Droz, 1975). Two Volumes.

AUTHOR INDEX

SUBJECT INDEX

About the Author

Charles H. Powers is an Assistant Professor in the Department of Anthropology and Sociology at Santa Clara University. In addition to writing several scholarly articles on the subject of Pareto for major American and European journals such as *Sociological Theory* and *Cahiers Vilfredo Pareto*, Dr. Powers edited the English translation of Pareto's final work, *The Transformation of Democracy*. His other work includes a number of articles on the structure of social roles, societal change, and the specification of useful theoretical principles for sociology. Dr. Powers is currently the editor of *Perspectives*, newsletter of the Theory Section of the American Sociological Association.

NOTES